To

From

God's by Grace i Stand

"By whom also we have access by faith into this grace wherein we stand and rejoice in hope of the glory of God."

Romans 5:2

By God's Grace I Stand

My Walk of Faith

Dr. Letitia McPherson

by God's Grace i Stand
PUBLISHER

By God's Grace I Stand

Copyright © 2024 by LETITIA MCPHERSON

All rights reserved. No part of this book may be reproduced or transmitted in any form or by any means without written permission from the author.

ISBN: 978-1-990266-61-4

Printed in the USA by Amazon

Other Books by Dr. Letitia McPherson

The Potter, The Clay, the Process

Facing the Storms of Life

Walking Through the Valley

From the Mouth of the Prophet

Table of Contents

Dedication	1
Foreword	5
Preface	7
Introduction	11
Chapter 1: The Foundation of Faith	15
Chapter 2: Early Life and Love	19
Chapter 3: Facing Early Fears	23
Chapter 4: Confronting Darkness	29
Chapter 5: Healing The Wounds	33
Chapter 6: A Save Haven	39
Chapter 7: Courage to Speak	45

Chapter 8:	Family Forgivness	51
Chapter 9:	Music As Medicine	55
Chapter 10:	The Power OF Song	61
Chapter 11:	A New Dawn	67
Chapter 12:	Embracing Faith	73
Chapter 13:	A Global Calling	77
Chapter 14:	Tribute	83
Chapter 15:	Answering The Call	87
Chapter 16:	A Global Mission	93
Chapter 17:	Overcoming Adversities	99
Chapter 18:	Rekindling the Flame of Faith	103
Chapter 19:	A Mother's Legacy	107
Chapter 20:	Manifesting God's Glory	111
Chapter 21:	Healing Through Faith	115
Chapter 22:	Finding Strength in Suffering	119
Chapter 23:	Ministry Beyond Time	123
Chapter 24:	Confrontation and Forgiveness	127
Conclusion:	A Legacy of Faith and Service	131

Sermons	**135**
Sermon # 1 Sermon	136
Sermon #2 God's Plan for Me	139
Sermon # 3 Rizpah and the Buzzards	143
Sermon # 4 Praise Him Through the Storm	147
Perspectives	**151**
Testimony by Vivienne - Gordon	171
Testimony of Edina M. Bayne	174
Sermon Notes - Nuggets	180

Dedication

> *...ye have done well, that ye have communicated with my afflictions, and my God shall supply all your needs according to His riches in glory by Christ Jesus.*
>
> **Romans 12:2**

To all who have bravely faced adversity, endured life's trials with unwavering faith, and shown that with God's grace, we can stand strong.

To Pastor Ann Marie Morris, your steadfast support and compassionate care from day one have been a blessing. Your grit and love have shone brightly, even in the most challenging moments.

While the journey has not always been smooth, God's grace has sustained our strength. This book is dedicated to you, a beacon of faith and inspiration.

To my beloved Citadel family, who have stood by me since our ministry's inception in Jamaica in 2004, your prayers and encouragement have fortified me. Your steadfast commitment ignites my passion every day. May your paths illuminate hope for all in search of faith and hope. We are a ministry founded on hope, faith, and love.

This dedication is for those who have also faced challenges and become stronger, showing determination and faith in God. Your strength and unwavering spirit inspire others. Keep demonstrating the amazing power of God's grace.

Letitia McPherson

>
>
> "May you find strength, hope, and renewed purpose through God's grace. Understand that a force greater than ourselves upholds us amidst life's challenges"

Foreword

I'm honoured to introduce you to "By God's Grace I Stand – My Walk of Faith." This book captures the profound journey of Bishop Dr. Letitia McPherson. Her path, shaped by unwavering faith and strength, showcases how belief in God can help us transcend even the darkest times.

This book shows the power of a life guided by faith. It's about facing and overcoming adversity. You'll find stories of struggle and triumph, all reflecting the power of hope.

Bishop Dr. Letitia McPherson is an ordinary person who faced extraordinary challenges. Her unwavering faith lit her path. Her story inspires everyone she meets.

I invite you to dive into this tale of courage and perseverance. Know that you are not alone in your journey. Whether you're facing trials or celebrating victories, let this book remind you that we stand by the grace of God.

As you read, let the incredible faith of this extraordinary woman touch your heart and soul. May you experience the transformative power of faith in God.

I hope "By God's Grace I Stand" leaves a lasting mark on your heart. May it inspire you to face life's trials with courage and faith.

With gratitude, Dr Mary Ann Small-Cousins, PhD

Preface

Therefore, we are always confident, knowing that, whilst we are at home in the body, we are absent from the Lord: (For we walk by faith, not by sight:) We are confident, I say, and willing rather to be absent from the body, and to be present with the Lord.

Corinthian 5:5-8

With a heart full of gratitude and humility, I warmly welcome you to this book. Here, you will find a testament to a life dedicated to faith, service, and spreading the gospel of Jesus Christ. Reflecting on my journey, I see the blessings, challenges, and divine interventions that have shaped who I am today.

I share these intimate aspects of my life because I strongly believe that our personal experiences have the power to inspire, encourage, and uplift others as they navigate their journeys of faith and life in Christ. Whether experiencing triumphs or facing difficult trials, I have come to understand the significance of sharing our stories. Our testimonies bear witness to the grace of God, and testifying to the strength of faith in the face of adversity has a profound impact.

In these chapters, you will read about moments of triumph and trial, divine encounters, struggles with doubt, joys of service, and challenges in ministry.

I hope you find what you are looking for in your own experiences, find solace during struggles, and remember that we are never alone on our faith journey.

As we explore faith and resilience together, may you find renewed hope, strengthened faith, and a deeper connection to God's presence.

May these words guide you in darkness, comfort you in sorrow, and remind you of God's limitless love and grace.

I am grateful for the chance to share my story with you. I pray it touches your heart, inspires your spirit, and draws you closer to Jesus Christ.

Heavenly Father, we thank You for the journey You have led us on and the stories You have woven into our lives. As we explore faith and hope in this book, may Your light guide us, Your love surround us, and Your truth lead us.

Give us the courage to face challenges with faith, the strength to overcome adversity, and the wisdom to see Your presence in every moment. May this book be a vessel of Your grace, bringing comfort, inspiration, and hope to all who read it. Bless each reader with Your abundant love and peace. May the words here testify to Your faithfulness and the power of Your grace.

In the Mighty Name of Your Son Jesus Christ, I pray, Amen!

With heartfelt gratitude and unwavering faith,
Letitia

Introduction

My Journey of Faith

---- 66 ----

But without faith it is impossible to please him: for he that cometh to God must believe that he is, and that he is a rewarder of them that diligently seek him.

Hebrews 11:6 kjv

---- 99 ----

In the Bible, the timeless promise of God echoes: "I will never leave you nor forsake you." This comforting assurance serves as a constant reminder of God's presence in our lives, guiding our paths and encouraging us to walk in unwavering faith.

Faith is a transformative journey that profoundly shapes our lives, even though we might not understand it. In trials and triumphs, we are called to trust the unseen, believing God rewards those who seek Him earnestly (Hebrews 11:6 KJV).

This book, "By God's Grace I Stand," shows the resilience of the life lived in the Holy Spirit. It highlights a life anchored in steadfast faith, demonstrating the power of trust in God, persistence, and an unyielding commitment to a divine calling.

These pages will share a story about a journey filled with bravery in tough times, strength during life's challenges, and finding comfort in faith in Jesus Christ.

This story is a testament to triumph over adversity, renewal of hope in times of despair, and strength drawn from faith in Jesus Christ. It shows how a life rooted in Christ can transform us and help us endure life's struggles.

In this book – "by God's Grace i Stand," we will explore the profound impact of living by faith through God's grace, the strength of a spirit-filled life, and the resilience of those who rise above their circumstances.

This story reminds us that we are never alone, even in our darkest times. As we journey through these pages together, may this story kindle hope in the hearts of those wrestling with challenges. Let it inspire, uplift, and empower you, reminding us all that by the grace of God, we stand firm!

I can do all things through Christ which strengthens me.

Chapter 1

The Foundation of Faith

Overcoming Early Challenges with Courage

> *Now faith is the substance of things hoped for, the evidence of things not seen.*
>
> **Hebrews 11:1**

In the tapestry of life, strands of faith intertwine to tell tales of bravery, resilience, and a steadfast commitment to a greater purpose. This chapter explores my journey in depth, a path marked by obstacles, victories, and the profound impact of faith during life's most challenging times.

My name is Letitia. From a young age, my grandmother's prophecy that I would be a light in the darkness, a voice of hope, and a vessel of grace amidst the turmoil has been a guiding force in my life. My life intertwines faith and service with experiences of pain, betrayal, love, and redemption. May my stories touch the hearts of those who read this book.

From my early years until now, I have lived and journeyed with the unwavering guidance of Jesus Christ. His presence has not only made my path possible, but also illuminated it with hope and grace.

My journey has taken me across diverse cultures and continents, driven by God's divine calling and anchored in His boundless love and grace. I have encountered life-and-death situations and adversity and achieved great heights in ministry and service in Jesus' name.

I extend an invitation to read this book, which provides an intimate portrayal of my life shaped by steadfast faith in Jesus Christ.

Together, we will explore the key moments that have shaped my character and given me a sense of purpose. From the strength gained through fasting, prayer, and the ever-present grace of God during times of healing and restoration, you will witness the profound experiences I have undergone.

These words will give you insight into my innermost thoughts, cherished dreams, and compassion for others. The strength shown in my story will inspire those who, like me, have faced challenging circumstances.

My story goes beyond personal victories. It embodies the biblical principles of grace, faith, hope, and love. It inspires us to walk the path of righteousness with courage, guided by Psalm 23:3.

Join me on this journey of revelation, introspection, and inspiration. Discover a life consecrated to God and His ministry, characterized by victories over adversities through God's grace and fueled by a passion to embrace the "globe with the gospel of Jesus Christ."

May my story shine as a guiding light in

darkness, a source of hope in despair, and a testament to the steadfastness of faith in adversity. Welcome to my journey of faith and resilience.

Chapter 2

Early Life and Love
Growing Up in Good Hope

Charity suffereth long and is kind; charity envieth not; charity vaunteth not itself, is not puffed up.

1st Cor 13:4

I entered this world on a leap day, February 29th, 1952, in Good Hope, Clarendon, Jamaica. My formative years were filled with love and the nurturing care of my grandmother, Beatrice. Growing up in Good Hope near Kellits, my childhood was filled with warmth and my grandmother's gentle embrace and love. Her home served as a sanctuary of comfort and familiarity, where I etched cherished memories under her tender guidance.

My mother's pursuit of employment in the city of Kingston necessitated my early days spent under my grandmother's care from birth, fostering a profound bond between us.

I felt wrapped in love from my earliest days in her humble country home. Despite the lack of modern conveniences like electricity and running water, life was simple and peaceful. Bathing in the river, using the outhouse as a toilet, and living without electricity were part of our daily lives in the 1950s. For a young child, it felt like heaven.

The smell of Grandma's home-cooked meals, especially her cornmeal porridge for breakfast, stewed chicken for dinner and cornmeal pudding or desert—oh Lord, her cornmeal pudding—was the essence of my childhood. The soothing bedtime songs and her comforting touch wove together the fabric of my early years.

In the fields of Good Hope, I found peace in the

simple paces of country life. Each day, I brought new adventures and discoveries.

From the serenity of home to the lively Good Hope market and gatherings with friends and family on market days, I learned about community and companionship. These experiences shaped the values that would guide me later in life.

Playing under the mango, orange, and ackee trees, I absorbed my grandma's wisdom and traditions, which had been passed down through generations. As a child this information grounded me in my heritage and gave me a strong sense of belonging.

My grandmother's stories became my bedtime tales, painting vivid pictures of family customs and cultural heritage. They deeply rooted me in my Jamaican lineage.

In her embrace, I found unconditional love and support. She was the cornerstone of my identity and values. Her presence guided me through life's uncertainties, shaping me into the person she knew I could become.

Chapter 3

Facing Early Fears
A Harsh Transition to a New Life

❝

You shall not be afraid of the terror by night, Nor of the arrow that flies by day, Nor of the pestilence that walks in darkness, Nor of the destruction that lays waste at noonday. A thousand may fall at your side, And ten thousand at your right hand, But it shall not come.

Psalm 91:5-8 nkjv

❞

During my formative years, my grandmother's cozy home in Good Hope was a sanctuary of safety and warmth. However, the tranquillity of those cherished memories was abruptly shattered by the devastating loss of my grandmother. She departed this world at the tender age of fifty from a heart attack, leaving an indelible void in my heart that echoed with grief and longing.

After her funeral, my mother decided that living with her in Kingston wasn't the best option. She chose to take me to live with my father in St. Catherine.

I felt immense heartbreak and disappointment. I had lost my anchor and now faced moving in with a father I barely knew.

The transition was sudden and harsh. I remember grappling with pain, disappointment, and fear as I began this new chapter of my life.

Leaving behind my cherished childhood memories, I held onto a flicker of hope as we travelled to my father's home in Lluidas Vale, St. Catherine.

The journey was terrifying for a young girl. The steep, winding roads, mountains, and potholes made it a frightening experience I'll never forget.

After what felt like hours, we reached Lluidas Vale. Though known for its beauty and agriculture, to me, it was a place where darkness and fear lurked everywhere.

Stepping into this new world, I felt anticipation, curiosity, and a lingering fear, like a heavy fog.

Living with my father introduced me to a new way of life, filled with unfamiliar routines, rules, and expectations.

Living with my father was a complex experience. I struggled to find my place in this new and strange environment. Sometimes, living with him might bring a brighter future - I thought. I felt a tiny spark of hope and a sense of belonging. However, I never imagined this hopeful transition would turn into a nightmare.

Over time, I began to adjust, forming bonds and making memories in my father's home. I found comfort in a caregiver who reminded me of my grandmother. Her smile, cooking, and warmth became a source of solace.

Yet, beneath this facade of normalcy, a dark secret waited to shatter my innocence. As weeks turned into months, I tried to adapt to life with my father. Despite his stern nature, I saw glimpses of his care for me.

I worked hard to be the daughter he wanted. I helped with chores and followed his rules. My sisters and I found joy and laughter in our backyard as we played together. I will refrain from further delving into my sisters' experiences as I aim to recount my journey. I hope that, in due time, they will summon the strength to share their own unique stories, and I am here to support their healing and growth.

But I couldn't ignore the tension and whispers of hidden truths. One day, the reality of our situation became clear. It was more sinister than anything I had imagined.

Faced with this new and dangerous chapter, I prepared myself for the journey ahead. Drawing on my inner strength, I was determined to navigate this harsh reality. Little did I know then that this phase of my life would shape me in unimaginable ways. It would propel me toward my true purpose and light the path to my destiny, just as my grandmother had prophesied.

Chapter 4

Confronting Darkness
Unveiling the Pain of Abuse

"For God hath not given us the spirit of fear; but of power, and of love, and of a sound mind."

2 Timothy 1:7

I recall the nights when my father would intrude into my room, I remember the instinct to curl into a protective ball, turning my back to the wall. I would pretend to be asleep, hoping he would leave. But he would stay, and his touch would become increasingly inappropriate, leaving a lasting impact.

At times, I found myself hiding under the bed, feeling scared and praying for the situation to end. These experiences shattered my trust and sense of safety with my father. What should have been a loving relationship turned into something terrible and violating, throwing me into a state of confusion so profound, it was like being lost in a maze of emotions and thoughts, and indescribable pain.

Over time, the shame and fear became too much to endure. I felt trapped and alone, suffocating under the weight of the secrets I was keeping.

Realizing the extent of the sexual and physical abuse I had suffered was a slow and excruciating process. Each resurfaced memory reminded me of how deeply I had been betrayed by the one person in my life who was supposed to protect me. The trauma my father inflicted left deep mental and physical scars that threatened to overwhelm me.

In my darkest moments, I discovered a wellspring of strength inside me. I faced my inner demons and confronted the shadows. With no one else to trust, I learned to talk to myself - the chickens in my father's chicken coup also became my trusted companions.

As I bravely confronted the painful truths, I began to break free from the suffocating silence that had held me captive, a process that was both liberating and empowering. This marked the beginning of my journey toward healing and rediscovering my voice—a voice that I had stifled for too long, a voice once vibrant and confident due to my grandma's influence but which had been silenced by my struggles.

"Fear thou not; for I am with thee: be not dismayed; for I am thy God: I will strengthen thee; yea, I will help thee; yea, I will uphold thee with the right hand of my righteousness." Isaiah 41:10 kjv

Chapter 5

Healing The Wounds

Coping with Abuse - Finding Strength in Despair

―――――――― ――――――――

"Be strong and of a good courage, fear not, nor be afraid of them: for the Lord thy God, he it is that doth go with thee; he will not fail thee, nor forsake thee."

Deuteronomy 31:6

―――――――― ――――――――

The abuses left scars on my body and soul. The pain, fear, and trauma became a part of who I am. The sexual abuse and physical violence took away my innocence and shattered my sense of self.

……The pain consumed me with fear, self-blame, despair, confusion, and condemnation because of my past. It threatened to wreck me!

It started when I was young. My father, who should have protected me, instead hurt and betrayed me. My childhood had been stolen, replaced by shame and confusion that suffocated me.

The wounds from my father, a respected religious man in our community, went beyond the physical. They cut deep into my soul, leaving scars no one could see.

The scars on my skin are nothing compared to the pain inside me, which consumed me with fear, self-blame, despair, confusion, and condemnation because of my past, threatening to wreck me.

Through enduring ongoing abuse, I became

entangled in a complex silent power struggle with my father, fighting fiercely for survival. The bruises and scars I bear are a testament to the silent battles waged within my father's home at night.

Dealing with the aftermath of the sexual and physical abuse was a constant battle. I was caught between feeling numb and being overwhelmed by my emotions. I built walls around my heart to protect myself from the world. But those same walls trapped me in a prison of pain and loneliness.

Even in my darkest moments, I held onto Psalm 56, which I learned in Sabbath school. It says, *"God, have mercy on me. People are trying to hurt me. My enemies attack me every day. When I am afraid, I put my trust in you. I praise God for his word. I trust in God, so I am not afraid of what people can do to me. They twist my words and plot against me. They get together and hide, watching my every step, hoping to kill me. God, punish them in your anger for their sin. You keep track of my pain. You collect my tears in your bottle and record them in your book. When I cry out to you, my enemies will retreat. I know this because God is on my side. I praise God for his word. I trust in the Lord. I am not afraid of what people can do to me. God, I will keep my promises to you. I will give you offerings of thanks. You have saved me from death. You have kept me from falling. So I will walk with God in the light of life."* (Psalm 56)

This scripture was deeply rooted in my heart, even as a child. It became my anthem as I struggled through the horrifying experiences of my teenage years. This passage gave me hope, faith, and strength. It sparked a defiance in me that refused to give up.

My journey to healing and freedom started with the brave choice to face my pain head-on. I remembered God's promise in Deuteronomy 31:6 - *"Be strong and courageous. Do not be afraid of them. The Lord your God goes with you. He will never leave you or abandon you."* Knowing this pushed me to get help and start putting the broken pieces of myself back together.

Philippians 4:13: "I can do all things through Christ which strengtheneth me"!

Chapter 6

A Safe Haven
Finding Solace in Benbow

---- ----

When thou passest through the waters, I will be with thee; and through the rivers, they shall not overflow thee: when thou walkest through the fire, thou shalt not be burned; neither shall the flame kindle upon thee.

Isaiah 43:2

----- 99 -----

As the storm raged within me, the weight of pain and despair pressed down on my young shoulders like a boulder. It felt like a burden too heavy to bear. In a moment of clarity amidst the chaos, I made a choice that would change my life forever - I ran! Yes I ran!

Leaving my father's home, I embarked on a journey of escape and survival, guided by an inner compass that led me to Benbow, a small district nestled in the hills of St. Catherine. It was a journey that tested my determination and courage.

Benbow is a community where life flows to the sounds of neighbours chatting over gates and children's laughter echoing through the air.

The sun casts its beautiful golden rays on the colourful houses lining Benbow Street, settling a sense of tranquillity over the neighbourhood. The scent of blooming bougainvillea mixes with the aroma of homemade meals wafting from kitchen windows, creating a picture of warmth and familiarity that instantly makes you feel welcomed and at home.

In the evenings, the street comes alive with music drifting from open windows and the glow of kerosene oil lamps lighting the pathways. Benbow was a place where everyone knew everyone, stories were shared, dreams were nurtured, and bonds and friendships were formed in a close-knit community.

In the heart of Benbow, every house holds a unique story—tales of overcoming challenges, experiencing both happiness and heartache and embodying strength and optimism. The echoes of the past share their wisdom with the present, while the future presents an array of promising opportunities.

"..... The scars of the past slowly began to fade. In their place, seeds of resilience and empowerment....."

As I walk the streets of Benbow, I am reminded of the enduring spirit of its residents, their strong sense of community, and the bond that ties them together. In the heart of Benbow, I find not just solace, but also a wellspring of inspiration amidst daily life. It is a sanctuary where memories are cherished, and dreams are born.

Benbow isn't just a district; it's a place where love stories are written, and the very essence of home is intricately woven into its every fiber. When I arrived, Benbow welcomed me with open arms, embracing me in a warm cocoon of solace during a tumultuous time in my life.

In this close-knit community, I found comfort with Missionary Wynter, a cherished figure from my childhood. She had been transferred to this district a few years earlier. Her warm embrace gave me hope and empathy. She soothed my body and spirit with eyes filled with understanding and a gentle touch. Her modest home became a sanctuary where I could begin to untangle the knots of pain and fear that had kept me bound.

Missionary Wynter ensured I received an education by enrolling me in school. My teacher, Ms. Gordon, was a wonderful and kind-hearted individual who embraced me wholeheartedly. Her love and support have left an indelible mark on my heart, and I will always cherish the impact she has had on my life.

Missionary Wynter's residence provided a nurturing environment for healing and rejuvenation. Within its walls, I could release the burdens of my past and piece together my fractured self. Her soothing words, counsel, and beautiful singing relieved my wounded spirit. Her presence reminded me that I was not alone in facing adversity.

In the tranquillity of Benbow, I embarked on a journey of self-restoration and exploration. It was a gradual process, as I uncovered layers of trauma, reclaiming my sense of self and identity. The wounds of years past began to fade, making way for new growth and strength, nurtured by Missionary Wynter's love, care, and unwavering support reminded me of God's word from Jeremiah 30:17.

"For I will restore health unto thee, and I will heal thee of thy wounds, saith the Lord; because they called thee an Outcast, saying, This is Zion, whom no man seeketh after." Jeremiah 30:17 (KJV)

Chapter 7

Courage to Speak
Sharing the Untold Truth

And ye shall know the truth, and the truth shall make you free.

John:32

The secrets I carried grew heavier daily, threatening to suffocate me in silence. The weight of my father's abuse haunted me, filling me with a toxic brew of shame, fear, and isolation. Each day, the burden seemed to carve deeper into my soul, creating wounds that festered in the shadows of my mind.

Desperate for a sanctuary, I sought solace in a small shed below Missionary Wynter's house, a place that offered a fragile semblance of safety.

"…..Wrapped in God's grace, I discovered a resilience that defied my pain and fear. ….."

Here, amidst the scent of old wood and rusted tools, my spirit drifted, yearning for the relief that seemed perpetually out of reach. The musty smell of the workshop, the rough and unforgiving texture of the wood, and the cold touch of the tools all seemed to conspire against me. In profound despair, I cried out to God for liberation, my voice echoing in the stillness. But the silence that followed felt like a void, amplifying my sense of abandonment.

During my most challenging moment, a faint spark of hope appeared. It seemed like a divine presence spoke to me, echoing my grandma's words: "You will be a beacon in darkness, piercing through the suffocating stillness." The voice encouraged me to break away from the shackles of silence and disgrace, urging me to tell my story and let the truth guide me toward recovery.

The thought was frightening, yet it also felt like a rope thrown to me—a guiding light in the deepest darkness. I was determined to tell my story and not be defeated; it was time to find my way out of darkness and into the light.

With trembling hands and a heart heavy with fear and determination, I took the first step. I spoke my truth to Missionary Wynter, confronting the ghosts that had haunted me for so long and revealing the deep wounds hidden within. Each word I uttered felt like a step toward my liberation, a small victory against the darkness that had consumed me.

Wrapped in God's grace, I discovered a resilience that defied my pain and fear. This journey became one of faith and courage, leading me toward freedom and wholeness. It was not an easy path; it was a path marked by moments of doubt, tears, and the painful process of reliving my trauma. But it was also a path illuminated by hope and the promise of healing.

I found the courage to open up to Missionary Wynter, the one person I learned to trust completely. Her presence was a balm to my wounded spirit, and her counsel helped lighten my burden. She listened without judgment, offering wisdom and compassion that began mending my soul's fractures. The darkness that had once engulfed me began to recede, replaced by a glimmer of light guiding me to healing. I encourage others to seek help, as it is a powerful step towards healing and growth.

Breaking the silence was much more than an act of courage; it was a testament to God's strength within me. It was a journey marked by God's grace, guiding me towards healing and empowerment.

By sharing my story, I discovered a renewed sense of purpose and self-worth that went beyond the torment I endured. Once crippled by fear, I came to realize that my voice had the power to inspire and uplift others who may be walking a similar path.

In the following days, I continued to speak my truth, each time feeling lighter and more accessible. I began to see the beauty in my resilience, the strength in my vulnerability. My journey was far from over, but I was no longer alone. I had God's grace, the support of Missionary Wynter, and the newfound strength within me to guide my way.

As I moved forward, I understood that my story was not just a tale of suffering but a testament to the power of faith, hope, and the unwavering spirit of a life lived in Christ. It was a story of redemption, of finding light in the darkest places. With each step, I knew I was walking toward a future filled with healing and promise.

"The Lord is nigh unto all them that call upon him, to all that call upon him in truth." Psalm 145:18 KJV

"I have no greater joy than to hear that my children walk in truth." 3rd John 1:4 KJV

"The bruises and scars bore witness to the silent battles I fought, struggling to survive in a world where safety and trust were distant memories."

Chapter 8

Family Forgiveness
The Complexities of Reunions

> *For our comely parts have no need: but God hath tempered the body together, having given more abundant honour to that part which lacked. That there should be no schism in the body; but that the members should have the same care one for another. And whether one member suffer, all the members suffer with it; or one member be honoured, all the members rejoice with it.*
>
> **1 Corinthians 12:24-26**

At 15, filled with gratitude for Missionary Wynter and a longing heart, I set out to find my mother in Kingston. The hope of reuniting with her guided me through the darkness that clouded my life.

With a crumpled slip of paper bearing my mother's address, given to me by my caregiver, when I ran away from my father's house.

".... His rage erupted, leading to a horrific act of violence....?

Kingston was a stark contrast to peaceful Benbow, pulsing with life.

I searched all day, asking strangers for directions, until a kind Samaritan offered me a ride. This stranger would become my lifelong friend and introduce me to gospel music—a talent I didn't know I had.

The reunion with my mother was a mix of joy and sorrow. After being apart for years, we embraced. Her presence both comforted and unsettled me, as I had only seen her a couple of times when I was a child - once at age 3 and then again at my grandmother's funeral. While at her home, I felt like I belonged, and it was a safe place to bond with my mother and start to understand my complicated past.

During the first few months of living and bonding with my mother, I felt free and ready to move forward with building a new life for the first time. However, the shadow of my father's abuse intruded on the fragile peace I had found.

His menacing presence intruded upon the sanctuary I sought, reminding me of the trauma that still haunted me.

One night, I was returning from an album recording session with friends when my father appeared unexpectedly without notice. His rage erupted, leading to a horrific act of violence where he smashed a bottle of overproof rum on my head, leaving broken glass and a bloody trail into my mother's house - the scar remains a painful reminder of his brutality.

The resumption of physical abuse was a harsh wake-up call, reminding me of the cycle of violence that had plagued my life. The bruises and scars bore witness to the silent battles I fought, struggling to survive in a world where safety and trust were distant memories.

As time passed, I struggled with the conflicting emotions of love and fear. My longing for the peace of Benbow was often overshadowed by the complexities of family ties and trauma. The path to healing and freedom grew more pressing by the day as I fought to break free from the shackles of abuse and rediscover my sense of self-worth and independence.

Chapter 9

Music As Medicine
Healing Through Harmony

> *But will sing of thy power; yea, I will sing aloud of thy mercy in the morning: for thou hast been my defence and refuge in the day of my trouble. Unto thee, O my strength, will I sing: for God is my defence, and the God of my mercy.*
>
> **Psalm 59:16-17**

Amidst the shadows of abuse and turmoil in Kingston, I managed to finish high school and get a job. However, my newfound hope and sense of security were shattered by workplace rape, pregnancy, and a miscarriage at age seventeen. Yet, I uncovered moments of light and comfort that offered healing. Amid family struggles and personal pain, I sought comfort in the warm embrace of a church community, where I found peace and a sense of belonging and support that I had longed for. The warmth and acceptance of fellow congregants eased the burdens on my heart.

Friendships in the church became pillars of support. Laughter and companionship offered strength and joy, reminding me I was not alone. There was hope even in the darkest moments.

Friends encouraged me to discover a hidden talent: singing. This discovery led me to music ministry, where I found a sense of purpose and fulfillment that transcended past traumas.

Singing songs of praise and worship became a source of healing and release for me. One song, *"In times like these we need a Savior. In times like these we need an anchor. Be very sure, be very sure Your anchor holds and grips the Solid Rock!"* became my daily refuge, offering comfort and consolation. Through its harmonies, I found a way to express my emotions and seek comfort in the resonating chords that echoed my innermost feelings.

Music became a way for me to connect with others by sharing my story through its powerful language. Despite my struggles, the moments in music ministry have brought joy and peace and, most importantly, revealed the profound beauty that can emerge from adversity. The stage became a sanctuary where I could share my voice and connect with others.

Years later, while in Kingston, I found that my talents extended beyond singing. I vividly remember the day I participated in a production with friends at the famous Randy Williams Theatre in New Kingston. It was there that I discovered my talent for acting, a moment that would change my life. I auditioned for the role of the plantation's wife and secured the part.

The production's success made me believe that acting was my true passion. However, over time, I realized that my heart was not fully invested in acting. I struggled to identify my true calling, despite my efforts. Little did I know that years later, I would uncover my God given passion for teaching and preaching His word.

"O sing unto the Lord a new song; for he hath done marvellous things: his right hand, and his holy arm, hath gotten him the victory." Psalm 98-104

(I dedicate this chapter to Joan Creary and the Creary sisters, who recognized and nurtured the gift of music within me.)

Letitia McPherson

> "...It was a daunting journey, often fraught with setbacks and moments of overwhelming despair..."

Chapter 10

The Power OF Song
Using Music to Overcome Trauma

Blessed be God, even the Father of our Lord Jesus Christ, the father of mercies, and the God of all comfort; Who comforteth us in all our tribulation, that we may be able to comfort them which are in any trouble, by the comfort wherewith we ourselves are comforted of God. For as the sufferings of Christ abound in us, so our consolation also aboundeth by Christ.

2 Corinthians 1:3-5

The violation of my body and spirit left wounds deeper than physical scars. These wounds entangled me in a web of shame, fear, and confusion, overshadowing the glimmers of hope, joy and light that occasionally pierced through the darkness.

The struggle between light and darkness became more pronounced as I sought solace amidst the chaos and faced the darkness threatening to engulf me.

At night, my soul was burdened by silenced secrets and muffled voices. The melodies that once brought comfort now echoed with anguish and grief, creating a battleground between trauma and the promise of God's healing. Each note seemed to carry the burden of my past, resonating with the pain that I struggled to articulate.

Amidst the turmoil, I clung to the flickers of resilience within me. I stood firm against the shadows, striving to liberate myself from the chains of abuse. Despite the relentless grip of adversity, I aimed to reclaim my voice and power. It was a daunting journey, often fraught with setbacks and moments of overwhelming despair, but the seeds of hope had been planted, and they began to take root.

"…Despite the scars and the pain, there was a part of me that remained unbroken …"

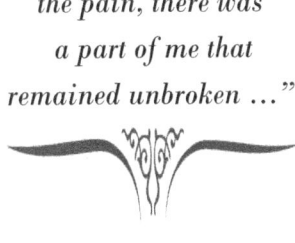

I found a wellspring of spiritual strength and courage in my internal struggle. I drew on God's grace to navigate the depths of trauma, discovering that within my pain lay a profound capacity for healing. Each step forward, no matter how small, was a testament to my faith in Jesus Christ and the strength that pushed me toward liberation.

I reached out to trusted individuals who became part of my support system. Among them was Missionary Wynter, whose wisdom and compassion provided a safe space for my wounded soul. Her guidance was instrumental in helping me untangle the knots of shame and fear that had bound me for so long. She reminded me that I was not alone and that God's love was a constant presence, even in my darkest hours.

As I continued to confront my past, I began to see the power of vulnerability. Sharing my story, though painful, became a source of empowerment. Each revelation, each confession, was a step toward reclaiming my narrative. I learned that my truth, once buried beneath layers of silence, had the power to inspire and heal—not just for myself but for others who might be walking a similar path.

The journey toward self-empowerment and healing was a testament to the role of faith in dispelling despair. It became a beacon of hope, a narrative redefined with each step. My path was illuminated by the enduring light of faith, a process that ebbed and flowed but grew stronger each day, dispelling the shadows that had long dominated my life.

In moments of quiet reflection, I found comfort and peace in prayer and meditation. These practices became a sanctuary where I could connect with the Lord and draw strength from a source greater than myself. I began to understand that true healing was not just about overcoming the past but embracing the present and looking forward to the future with hope and anticipation.

I also found solace in creative expression—writing, acting, and music became outlets for my emotions, allowing me to process my pain in a constructive way. These creative efforts became a bridge between my inner turmoil and the healing light that was gradually transforming my life. They helped me to articulate the inexpressible, to give form to the formless wounds within me.

During this journey, I made a fascinating discovery: the profound resilience of the human spirit. Despite the scars and the pain, a part of me remained unbroken - a core of strength that refused to die. This resilience was a testament to God's divine fire within me, reflecting His steadfast love and grace.

My journey was far from over, but I understood that healing was a lifelong process. It is a continuous journey of growth and self-discovery. With each step, I move closer to a place of wholeness and peace, guided by faith and the enduring light of hope.

As I looked back on my journey, I saw not just

the pain and struggle but also the triumphs and moments of grace. I saw a narrative of resilience and empowerment, a story of a soul that steadfastly refused to be defined by its wounds. This refusal, this unwavering strength, is a testament to the power within each of us. With each new day, I continued to forge a path illuminated by the light of faith, hope, and divine love.

Let the heavens be glad and the earth rejoice; let the sea resound, and all that fills it. Psalm 96:11

Chapter 11

A New Dawn

Reinventing Life in Toronto

"Heal me, LORD, and I will be healed; save me and I will be saved, for you are the one I praise."

Jerimiah 17:14

My mother's move to Toronto was a significant moment in our family's history, a decision that would have a lasting impact on our lives. As a teenager left behind in Kingston, I took on the responsibility of caring for my younger brother and sister. It was a heavy burden for someone my age, but I accepted the challenge with love and determination.

The experience forced me to mature quickly, developing resilience and strength that would shape my future.

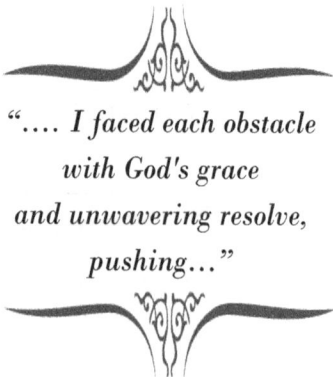

".... I faced each obstacle with God's grace and unwavering resolve, pushing..."

Toronto represented hope and new opportunities. Leaving Kingston behind was both exciting and scary. The idea of starting fresh in a big city like Toronto filled me with hope, making my past struggles seem a little less overwhelming.

When I arrived in Toronto at 19, it was a momentous moment in my life. I left Kingston's familiar comforts and challenges behind and embarked on a journey of growth and self-discovery. The city's diverse cultures and countless experiences weren't just a backdrop, they were a reflection of my own story, resonating deeply with the resilience that had carried me through numerous trials. The skyscrapers seemed to touch the sky just as my aspirations began to take flight.

".... Looking back, I see a journey of courage, faith, and an unwavering spirit ..."

Reuniting with my mother brought a profound sense of connection and renewal. Toronto's bustling streets became the backdrop for new possibilities, where I could dream and aspire freely. The city's energy was infectious, and I was invigorated by the endless opportunities that lay before me.

Adapting to a new culture and environment stirred a complex mix of emotions: excitement, anxiety, hope, and uncertainty. Despite the challenges, I faced each obstacle with God's grace and unwavering resolve, pushing forward with faith as my guiding light. Toronto's cultural mixture mirrored my journey, painting a picture of struggles and triumphs woven together by the thread of resilience.

In Toronto, I embraced every opportunity for growth and self-discovery. The city became a catalyst for transformation, allowing me to let go of the past and embrace a new era. Education was a cornerstone of my journey. I enrolled in college, took a course to become a flight attendant, and even attended modelling school. Each milestone symbolized my commitment to personal growth, the resilience that guided me through adversity, and my determination to create a better future.

In Toronto, significant milestones marked my new beginnings. In 1974, my daughter Paula was born, filling my life with a profound love and purpose that I had never experienced before. Her arrival was a beacon of hope, reminding me of life's beauty and potential despite its challenges. In 1979, I married David, who brought stability and companionship into my life. Later that year, our son, David Jr., was born, completing our family and adding to the joy and kinship that defined our new journey.

The new life I was now experiencing filled my life with love, kinship, and the joy of watching my family thrive as we embarked on a journey of hope and reinvention. Each day in Toronto brought me closer to healing and wholeness, illuminated by my family's love and the grace of God. Once an intimidating maze of steel and glass, the city's skyline now stood as a testament to the endless possibilities ahead.

As I navigated the challenges and embraced the opportunities of my new life, I found that Toronto was more than just a city—a symbol of my resilience and a testament to God's transformation power. The experiences and milestones I encountered here became the building blocks of my identity, shaping me into a stronger, more empowered individual.

Looking back on my past, I see a journey marked by courage, faith, and an unyielding spirit.

Moving to Toronto was more than just a change in my physical location; it represented a profound transformation of my entire being. It marked a shift from darkness to light, from despair to hope, and from mere survival to a life of thriving. With each step I took in this vibrant city, I wholeheartedly embraced life's endless possibilities.

I had no idea that moving to Toronto was not just a change of address. It was a significant part of God's plan to guide me toward my purpose and destiny, helping me overcome the trauma that had once held me captive.

Chapter 12

Embracing Faith
The Start of a Spiritual Journey

"For I know the plans I have for you," declares the Lord, "plans to prosper you and not to harm you, plans to give you hope and a future."

Jeremiah 29:11

In 1980, a transformative divine intervention reshaped my life. I surrendered my life entirely to the Lord, embracing faith and experiencing a spiritual rebirth. This pivotal decision brought profound changes, such as changing my mindset about the reasons for wanting a life of my own, seeking revenge and forgiveness, redefining my existence and illuminating a new path involving walking a path of righteousness.

Surrendering to the Lord was a significant step for me. It meant relinquishing the need to control everything and embracing humility. I opened myself to God's guidance, which brought me a deep sense of peace and freedom. It was as if a heavy burden had been lifted from my shoulders, and I was now ready to move forward with a clear sense of purpose, guided by God's peace.

After I surrendered to the Lord, I was baptized in water. This was a symbolic way of showing that I was starting fresh and finding new hope. The act of being in the water symbolized a new beginning, like being reborn with the support of faith in Jesus Christ and His divine grace.

My old man was submerged in the baptismal water, and a new creation emerged, clothed in righteousness and hope. Salvation and baptism energized my spirit and kindled divine love in my heart.

As I emerged from the water after my baptism, I felt a fresh start and a new purpose. The support of newfound friends, faith, and the power of prayer strengthened my connection to God, bringing me hope, strength, and a deep sense of peace. This reassurance and comfort encouraged me to continue my spiritual journey with renewed energy and excitement.

My moment of surrender and water baptism marked a significant turning point in my life. It ushered in a new era of faith, restoration, and contentment. The person God created me to be unveiled in my new life in Jesus Christ, igniting a journey toward wholeness, joy and peace. This new era of faith brought a deep sense of restoration, healing past wounds, and a profound contentment that I had never experienced before.

That night, I was baptized with the Holy Spirit, and the evidence of speaking in tongues illuminated my path with God's love, grace, and power, igniting me with a deep sense of reassurance and comfort for the future.

"…Whom having not seen, ye love; in whom, though now ye see him not, yet believing, ye rejoice with joy unspeakable and full of glory…" 1st Peter 1:8

Chapter 13

A Global Calling
Taking Faith Across Borders

> *"By faith Abraham, when he was called to go out into a place which he should after receive for an inheritance, obeyed; and he went out, not knowing whither he went."*
>
> **Hebrews 11:8**

Amidst my spiritual journey, marked by surrender and baptism, I felt a deep calling to share the gospel of Jesus Christ globally.

Despite life's challenges, including a devastating divorce that left my two children and me heartbroken, the call to spread the message of forgiveness, love, and salvation became clear.

Even after facing life's challenges, such as the heartbreaking divorce from David in 1991, which affected me and my two children, I felt a strong calling to spread the message of forgiveness, love, and salvation.

"...The call to "embrace the globe with the gospel" compelled me to step out of my comfort zone..."

Three years after the divorce, a new chapter began when I met and married Paul, a profound preacher, teacher of the word, and accomplished musician, bringing a renewed sense of hope and love into our lives.

Our union brought joy and fulfillment. We spent many happy years together, spreading the gospel of Jesus Christ worldwide until he passed away in 2017, leaving me.

During the years of our marriage, Paul and I relocated to the vibrant city of Montreal, Quebec, where our ministry took on a whole new level of significance. Over three remarkable years, I had the privilege of witnessing an incredible outpouring of the Holy Spirit. It was awe-inspiring as more than 200 individuals underwent a profound spiritual transformation, embracing a new life in Christ through spiritual rebirth, baptism, and receiving the Holy Spirit.

This period deeply reaffirmed and strengthened my divine calling to share the gospel and to serve as a conduit for God's boundless love and grace. It was an invaluable experience that enriched my understanding of ministry and our collective spiritual journey, contributing significantly to our personal growth and spiritual journey.

After living in Montreal for three years, Paul and I felt called to start a ministry in the United States. Following the Lord's prompting, we moved to the USA, witnessing God's power at work among His people. The establishment of a new church and the impact of our ministry in the United States demonstrated God's faithfulness and provision.

The call to "embrace the globe with the gospel of Jesus Christ" motivated me to step out of my comfort zone and venture into unfamiliar territories to share the message of Jesus Christ.

This journey of embracing the gospel has been a catalyst for personal growth, developing a burning passion within me and compelling me to become a source of hope and healing for those needing forgiveness and comfort.

As I continued my global ministry, my heart overflowed with purpose. I travelled far and wide to share Christ's love and grace. I carried the mandate to make disciples of all nations (Matthew 28:18-20) and to be a vessel of God's compassion and mercy.

During our travels worldwide, my team and I shared the gospel of Jesus Christ - a message of faith, love, and hope - with people suffering and seeking a better way of life. Despite differences in language and culture, we spread the message of Jesus Christ's forgiveness, love, and healing to every village, city, and town, capturing the hearts of thousands everywhere.

Through my international ministry, I have become a living testament to the power of the Christian gospel and God's redemptive grace. My journey has demonstrated the power of faith, hope, and love to overcome barriers and bring healing to a world in need of God's grace and love.

Chapter 14

A tribute to Rev. Dr Paul A. McPherson (1958-2017)

Honouring a Partner in Faith

---   ---

So, ought men to love their wives as their own bodies. He that loveth his wife loveth himself.

Ephesians 5:28

"He who finds a wife finds a good thing and receives favor from the Lord."

Proverbs 18:22

---   ---

As I look back on the profound journey of faith and ministry that my beloved husband, Rev.

Dr. Paul A. McPherson, and I embarked on together, I am deeply grateful for his lasting impact on my life and so many others. Since we exchanged vows, Paul's unwavering commitment to serving the Lord alongside me has been a constant source of strength and inspiration.

Together, we answered God's call to spread the message of hope, love, and redemption. We travelled through different countries and cultures to fulfill our mission. Paul's musical talents, a gift from God, and his compassionate spirit, a reflection of His grace, enriched our ministry, touching the hearts, especially the hearts of the young people, in profound ways.

Paul's steadfast faith and commitment to the gospel shone brightly in every step, guiding others. He was a beacon of light in dark times, a source of comfort in trials, and a testament to God's transformative love.

Throughout our years of ministry, Paul's gentle guidance and support were my strength. His wisdom helped us navigate challenges, and his love touched countless lives needing healing and restoration.

In 2017, Paul transitioned to be with the Lord, raising his hands in thanksgiving. He left behind a legacy of faith and devotion. His memory lives on in the hearts of those who knew him as a friend, musician, pastor, and teacher. But to me, he was more than that. He was a loving husband, and his love and devotion to his family was unparalleled. He inspired us to continue spreading God's love and grace.

I dedicate this chapter to my beloved husband, Rev. Dr. Paul A. McPherson, in loving memory. We honour his legacy of music, faith, love, and service. May his spirit continue to guide and inspire us as we share the message of hope and redemption through our work."

Chapter 15

Answering The Call
A Commitment to Serve

❝

"You are the light of the world. A city set on a hill cannot be hidden. Nor do people light a lamp and put it under a basket, but on a stand, and it gives light to all in the house. In the same way, let your light shine before others, so that they may see your good works and give glory to your father who is in heaven."

Matthew 5:14–16

❞

After I experienced salvation and grew spiritually, I felt a strong call from the Lord to enter ministry. This call filled me with a deep sense of mission and purpose, guiding me toward a new chapter of faith and dedication.

"...God's presence was a constant source of comfort and encouragement, reminding me that I was never alone in this journey..."

The Lord's call to ministry was an invitation and a clear directive to serve as a leader. I was to spread grace, compassion, and hope to others. Living out the teachings of Christ and sharing His good news felt like a privilege and an awesome responsibility.

Obeying and following the Lord's call brought newfound clarity and purpose to my life. My path felt illuminated by divine guidance, wisdom, and understanding. It was as if God's light showed me the way forward, helping me navigate this new journey.

To begin the journey of ministry, one must possess faith, obedience, and dedication. It entails following the example of the Master with humility and grace. Each step taken demonstrates my commitment to answering the call and my readiness to serve God and His people.

As I embarked on this path, I realized that ministry was more than just preaching or teaching. It was about being there for others, offering a listening ear, a helping hand, and a compassionate heart. I wanted to be a vessel of God's love, reaching out to those in need and offering them hope and encouragement.

In my journey through ministry, I have experienced significant personal growth. I have dug deeper into the study of God's word, attended seminars, and sought guidance from experienced leaders. Every day, my aim has been to expand my knowledge and understanding of God's word and His plan for my life."

There were challenges along the way, moments

of doubt and uncertainty. But through prayer and faith, I found the strength to keep moving forward. God's presence was a constant source of comfort and encouragement, reminding me that I was never alone in this journey.

Serving in ministry has brought me many rewarding experiences. I have seen lives transformed by the power of God's love and grace. Witnessing the profound joy and peace that fills people's hearts when they accept Christ has been precious, and it has reinforced my commitment to the ministry and my belief in the gospel's transformative power.

Through it all, I remained committed to serving with humility and grace. It was about being a faithful servant dedicated to spreading His message of love and salvation.

Looking back on my past, I realize how rewarding it was to answer the call to ministry. This decision not only filled me with a deep sense of purpose and fulfillment but also led me on a journey marked by unwavering commitment to serve the

Lord and His people. It was a transformative journey that brought moments of deep faith, sacrifices, personal growth, and a profound dedication to my calling, demonstrating my unwavering commitment.

Forasmuch as yet know that ye were not redeemed with corruptible things, as silver and gold, from your vain conversation received by tradition from your fathers; But with the precious blood of Christ, as of a lamb without blemish and without spot: Who verily was foreordained before the foundation of the world, but was manifest in these last times for you, Who by him do believe in God, that raised him up from the dead, and gave him glory; that your faith and hope might be in God. Who by him do believe in God, that raised him up from the dead, and gave him glory; that your faith and hope might be in God. 1 Peter 1:18-21 kjv

Chapter 16

A Global Mission
Faith Across Continents

Be anxious for nothing, but in everything, with supplication and thanksgiving, make your requests made known to God and the peace that passes all understanding will guard your hearts and minds in Christ Jesus.

Philippians 4:6-7

My global mission is a journey of joy and faith. In Australia, I was moved by the resilience and deep spiritual connection of the

Aboriginal people to their land. In Kenya, the joy and faith of the Maasai tribe, despite their poverty and hardship, was a beacon of hope. In Nigeria, the local churches' vibrant worship and community spirit, despite their political and social conditions, was a source of inspiration."

"...I am in awe, with a sense of purpose and gratitude for the opportunity to serve God and humanity in such a profound way..."

In South Africa, I stood in awe of the reconciliation and forgiveness that took place after years of apartheid. In my lifetime, I had the privilege of visiting Israel four times; I felt the weight of history and faith in every step. Each journey is a profound spiritual pilgrimage. Walking in Jesus's footsteps, I was drawn to the Garden

Tomb twice. Words fail to capture the depth of my experience within those hallowed walls; it was a moment beyond the natural, a brush with the supernatural that defies explanation.

During my time in the United States, the diverse Christian community moved me with its infectious laughter and joy for life. Their love for family and the church family was so strong, it made me feel connected to a larger community. I witnessed and ministered in worship services where people from different cultural and racial backgrounds came together in the name of Christ. These experiences reinforced my belief in the unifying power of faith.

During my travels, I was deeply moved by the natural beauty of Canada, from its majestic mountains to its serene lakes. The locals in various Canadian provinces, including British Columbia, Saskatchewan, Quebec, Newfound Land, New Brunswick, Manitoba and Ontario, taught me lessons of humility and kindness. In the United Kingdom, I observed the enduring influence of centuries-old Christian traditions and the church's strength in a secular society. In the West Indies, I was embraced with open arms and experienced the warmth and enthusiasm of Caribbean worship.

These experiences have truly left an indelible mark on me, shaping my understanding of God's kingdom and reinforcing the importance of cultural sensitivity, humility, and the power of unity in diversity. They have also taught me how to embrace the beauty of God's creation in all its forms.

It's truly awe-inspiring to continue this global mission with a profound sense of purpose and gratitude for the opportunity to serve both God and humanity. I have been deeply humbled by the faith and resilience of the people I've encountered on this journey. Their unwavering commitment to serving God and spreading the gospel of Jesus Christ has been a great source of inspiration for me.

Ultimately, my global mission is not just about travelling to different countries and sharing my faith. It is about building bridges, breaking down barriers, and bringing people together in love and unity. It is about witnessing God's transformative power and grace in a world so often divided and broken.

And so, I press on with renewed determination and faith, knowing that the journey ahead may be challenging, but the reward of seeing lives changed and broken hearts mended is worth every pain, trial and tribulation. May my global mission continue to be a testament to the power of God's love and the hope of a brighter future for all.

Blessed are ye, when men shall revile you, and persecute you, and shall say all manner of evil against you falsely, for my sake. Rejoice, and be exceeding glad: for great is your reward in heaven: for so persecuted they the prophets which were before you. Yè are the salt of the earth: but if the salt have lost his savour, wherewith shall it be salted? it is thenceforth good for nothing, but to be cast out, and to be trodden under foot of men

Chapter 17

Overcoming Adversities
Triumphing Over Illness

> *So, you shall serve the Lord your God, and He will bless your bread and your water. And I will take sickness away from the midst of you. No one shall suffer miscarriage or be barren in your land; I will fulfil the number of your days.*
>
> **Exodus 23:25-26 kjv**

Both physical and spiritual challenges mark the story of my life. From 1983 to 2020, I faced many health issues that tested my faith and resilience.

Between 1983 and 1988, I underwent eight major surgeries. Each surgery was a battle, with skilled surgeons working to save my life. My faith in God's healing power strengthened me through these dark times.

In 1990, I faced heart disease, which was challenging, but my faith and determination helped me fight for my life and well-being.

In 1993, I was diagnosed with a brain tumour. Doctors gave me only three months to live. Yet, through divine grace, I experienced a miraculous healing that defied medical explanation. It was a testament to the power of faith and God's grace and mercy.

During these battles, a C-section led to bowel obstructions and two bowel resections. Another hospitalization resulted in a coma for three days after being given the wrong blood type. These trials tested my physical and emotional endurance. My rare AB Rh blood type made the situation even more dangerous.

Despite these challenges, my faith remained my guiding light. Each health crisis shaped my spirit and strengthened my resolve to face each challenge with unwavering faith in Jesus Christ.

My journey through these health challenges is a testament to God's grace that kept me and helped me to endure and overcome. Through suffering, I found resilience rooted in faith and belief in God's intervention. The scars from these battles tell a story of perseverance, courage, and hope, guiding my way through life's darkest moments.

"...Through adversity, I emerged not as a victim but as a warrior..."

Each trial became a stepping stone toward a deeper understanding of life's fragility and resilience. These challenges taught me about personal strength and the transformative power of faith, love, and hope.

Armed with faith, resilience, and unwavering

hope, I was able to navigate through life's challenges. My journey through physical and spiritual trials sculped a narrative of triumph over adversity.

As my life story unfolds, I embrace each trial as a chance for growth and change. These experiences reinforce my belief that the life lived by faith can overcome even the toughest challenges.

No weapon that is formed against thee shall prosper; and every tongue that shall rise against thee in judgment thou shalt condemn. This is the heritage of the servants of the Lord, and their righteousness is of me, saith the Lord. Isaiah 54:17

Chapter 18

Rekindling the Flame of Faith

Revival In Jamaica

———— 66 ————

What doth it profit, my brethren, though a man say he hath faith, and have not works? can faith save him?

James 2:14-26

———— 99 ————

My ministry in the West Indies began in the late 1980s, but my heart longed to return to Jamaica, the root of my spiritual journey.

As an evangelist, I felt called to spread the gospel

of Jesus Christ globally. I returned to Kingston, invited by the late Rev. Cedric Lue, who is now with God. May his soul rest in peace.

"...Divine providence led me back to where my deepest hurts began..."

My return to the land of my birth brought me to the Glad Tidings Open Bible Church in Spanish Town, St. Catherine, where Rev. Lue was the Pastor. He asked me to be the main speaker at their youth conference. Originally planned for three days, the convention extended into a powerful three-week-long spiritual awakening.

As a young minister, I was in awe of the divine events that unfolded during these gatherings. Many young people crowded the altar to show their love and reverence for God, praying, crying, worshiping and enjoying the presence of a most holy God.

Many people fully committed their lives to the Lord and were baptized as a earth shaking revival spread through the church and community, affecting the lives of everyone present.

People came from the four corners of the island to witness this revival, experiencing the tangible presence of God and the power of faith.

The air shook with a spiritual awakening as we embraced a revival that Spanish Town had never seen. All glory belongs to God, whose divine plan brought grace and redemption among us.

After the Spanish Town revival, the Holy Spirit led me to return to a place I had vowed never to revisit—Lluidas Vale. This place held painful memories of childhood trauma and abuse. Despite my reluctance, I answered the Lord's call.

Our first crusade in the marketplace of Lluidas Vale drew large crowds. Every night, the busy market overflowed with people, and over 200 souls surrendered to the Lord and were baptized in water, following Matthew 28:19-20.

A revival ignited the town, leading to the birth

of a new church and planting seeds of faith. A year later, a team from Toronto returned with me to Lluidas Vale, and we erected a tent for another crusade. We witnessed God's power and grace in the same town where my childhood wounds occurred. , to save my soul and guide me toward my divine destiny.

The district was astonished when the young girl, who had previously run away, returned with a powerful message of salvation, hope, and forgiveness, leaving everyone puzzled. No one knew why I had left or what had caused my transformation, but the impact of my ministry was undeniable, leaving a lasting impression on all who encountered it.

Jesus returned to Galilee in the power of the Spirit, and news about him spread through the whole countryside. He was teaching in their synagogues, and everyone praised him Luke 4:14.

Chapter 19

A Mother's Legacy

Honouring A Prayer Warrior

> "Let us therefore come boldly unto the throne of grace, that we may obtain mercy, and find grace to help in time of need."
>
> **Hebrews 4:16**

Since my ministry began in 1981 in the basement of our house, my mother was my greatest supporter and encourager. Her unwavering faith and dedication to the Lord guided me and inspired me to spread the gospel of Jesus Christ.

In 1990, my mother experienced a spiritual rebirth, and I had the pleasure of baptizing her in water. Her decision follow Christ marked a profound moment of growth and transformation in her life. Her commitment to prayer became a cornerstone of our ministry, as she fervently prayed for our work and those we served.

Her prayers provided strength and protection, guiding us through trials with unwavering faith and trust in God's plan. Losing my mother in 2001 at the age of 70 to non-Hodgkin lymphoma was one of the darkest days of my life.

I mourned the passing of my beloved mother and felt the loss of a dedicated prayer warrior. Her absence left a void in our ministry, as her prayers had been a pillar of support and guidance.

Reflecting on her legacy, I remember her unwavering faith, selfless dedication, and profound impact on those who knew her. Her memory lives on in the hearts of all was touched by her love and prayers. Her spirit inspires us to continue sharing God's love and grace.

Letitia McPherson

I dedicate this chapter in loving memory to my beloved mother, a prayer warrior and intercessor. I honour her life, faith, and tireless devotion to the Lord and the ministry. May her life of faith continue to guide and inspire us as we strive to fulfill the mission she held dear: spreading the message of hope, love, and redemption to all in need.

"Behold, everyone who uses proverbs will use this proverb about you: 'Like mother, like daughter.' Ezekiel 44:4 "Honor your father and your mother, that your days may be long in the land that the Lord your God is giving you. Exodus 20:12

Chapter 20

Manifesting God's Glory
Signs, Wonders and Miracles

> *And the Lord said unto Moses, I will do this thing also that thou hast spoken: for thou hast found grace in my sight, and I know thee by name. And he said, I beseech thee, shew me thy glory. And he said, I will make all my goodness pass before thee, and I will proclaim the name of the Lord before thee; and will be gracious to whom I will be gracious, and will shew mercy on whom I will shew mercy*
>
> **Exodus 33:17-22 kjv**

After my mother's passing, Paul and I returned to the United States to strengthen believers before moving back to Canada in 2003. Upon returning to Canada, I felt God's unmistakable call to return to Jamaica for an all-island crusade. Following a time of fasting and prayer, we set out on a mission to Kingston, Jamaica.

I preached salvation, hope, and faith in local churches, witnessing God's powerful presence in every service. Signs, wonders, and miracles were common, transforming lives, healing bodies, and mending hearts.

A remarkable event occurred when a man, who had been pronounced dead by doctors, was taken to a service in Kingston. With God's intervention, I shared words of faith with him and directed the individuals performing the baptism to take him to the water. They did so, baptized him, and as he emerged from the water, he was liberated by the Holy Spirit. He is now serving as a pastor in the United States.

The impact of the crusade reached Duhaney Park, where we organized a six-week event. During this period, 286 individuals were baptized, Citadel of Hope Ministries Jamaica was established, and the Duhaney Park community experienced a transformation through the power of the Holy Spirit.

Individuals who had previously threatened my life as part of a gang surrendered their weapons and their lives - embracing a new way of life. Despite facing challenges and threats, the Lord brought peace to the community, which has remained until today.

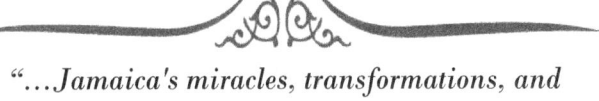

"...Jamaica's miracles, transformations, and divine encounters testified to God's unfailing power and ability to bring light and hope to even the darkest places..."

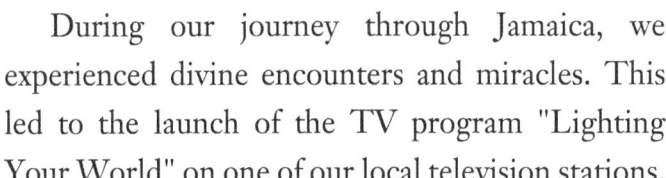

During our journey through Jamaica, we experienced divine encounters and miracles. This led to the launch of the TV program "Lighting Your World" on one of our local television stations.

The program became the number one religious program in the nation for three years. Souls were delivered and set free, displaying God's transformative power from Kingston to St. Andrew, St. Catherine to Clarendon, and beyond.

Amid challenges and triumphs, one truth remained steadfast—by God's grace, I stood. Through trials and victories in Duhaney Park and beyond, I found solace in Romans 5:2, *rejoicing in the hope of God's glory as His grace carried me through each step.*

Jamaica's miracles, transformations, and divine encounters testified to God's unfailing power and ability to bring light and hope to even the darkest places.

Chapter 21

Healing Through Faith
A Testament of God's Grace

---   ---

I shall not die, but live, and declare the works of the Lord.

Psalm 118:17

---   ---

Psalm 118:17 became more than words to me; it guided me through my health challenges. Born with rheumatic fever but diagnosed much later, I faced trials that tested my faith and resilience.

In 1982, a hospital visit for abdominal pain revealed a heart murmur linked to childhood rheumatic fever. Memories of being ill but untreated came back, with my grandmother's herbal remedies as our only care.

From 2011 to 2019, I faced five heart attacks and thirteen strokes. In 2015, during my time in Trinidad and Tobago as a guest minister at three churches, I experienced one heart attack and seven strokes within three days. It was a challenging time, but I faced it with courage, resulting in an 11-day hospital stay in both public and private hospitals. After undergoing extensive tests, the doctors recommended further evaluation in Canada upon discharge.

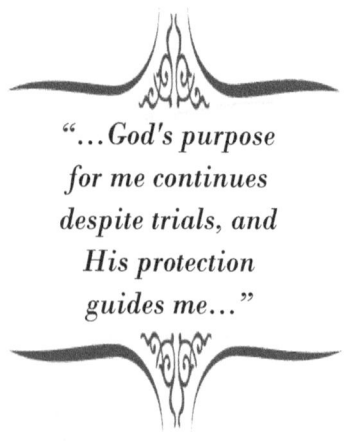

"...God's purpose for me continues despite trials, and His protection guides me..."

I opted out of returning to Canada and travelled to Jamaica instead.

I returned to Jamaica and had three more strokes three months later - one of those strokes was an eye stroke, causing me to lose sight in my right eye.

Each episode showed life's fragility and the need for unwavering faith. Through recovery, I held onto Psalm 118:17: *"I shall not die, but live, and declare the works of the Lord."* Through this challenging journey, I've learned firsthand the power of faith to sustain us through the toughest

In early 2020, I underwent surgery on my left carotid artery after experiencing multiple strokes and heart attacks. This surgery marked a significant turning point in my life. In the operating room, the combination of faith and science worked together for my restoration and brought hope for the future.

Prior to receiving anesthesia, I sang "The Goodness of God," a song that had been my source of strength since my 11th stroke. The lyrics served as a reminder of God's faithfulness in difficult times, bringing me peace and reassurance as I prepared myself for surgery.

Surviving these health challenges is a testament to God's grace and plans for my life. It reminds me that God's purpose for me continues despite trials, and His protection guides me.

As I moved forward in life, I held onto the life-changing promise of God that was spoken to me in 1992 by Pastor Jennifer Brown from Millville, New Jersey, during her visit to Revivaltimes Tabernacle in Toronto: *"You shall not die but live to declare the works of God."* This word has been more than an anchor; it has been a powerful force that provided unwavering assurance to navigate life's storms. God's faithfulness and promises sustain and uplift me. Romans 8:18 reminds me that today's trials pale compared to the eternal glory awaiting those who trust the Lord.

Chapter 22

Finding Strength in Suffering
Hope Amidst Afflictions

Many are the afflictions of the righteous: but the Lord delivered him out of them all.

Psalm 34:19

In moments of deep reflection, I turned to Psalm 34:19, "Many are the afflictions of the righteous, but the LORD delivers them out of them all." These words, speaking to the universal nature of suffering, resonated with me, offering hope amid my struggles through the Lord Jesus Christ.

As I walked through the valleys of life, I take comfort in Christ's teachings and his life as an example. His journey, marred by betrayal and crucifixion, is a beacon of strength in times of suffering. Though my trials cannot compare to His, His enduring love and grace provide me with a profound sense of reassurance, assuring me that I am not alone in my struggles.

Sharing my story with you reminds me of Jesus's life, and I realize that my struggles are part of a broader narrative of faith, purpous and perseverance. The path of righteousness often includes trials but also leads to a deeper understanding of God's faithfulness and deliverance. Walking in His footsteps, I found renewed purpose and trust in His plan for my life, a trust that brings reassurance and peace even in the face of my struggles.

"…sharing in Christ's suffering is a part of my faith journey…"

Inspired by King David's wisdom, I discovered the importance of finding peace and trust amidst turmoil and challenges. His life showed me that difficulties are not a sign of forsakenness but a chance for spiritual development and closeness to the Lord.

Through the years, in my daily quiet times, I felt His reassuring presence guiding me through life's challenges, providing grace, comfort and peace when I needed it most.

The words of 1 Peter 4:12-13 struck a chord with me, reminding me that sharing in Christ's suffering is part of my spiritual journey. While my hardships may not compare to His, they deepen my faith and commitment to His teachings. Embracing trials as opportunities for growth and change, I discovered a renewed sense of purpose and tranquillity in His embrace.

If my journey resonates with you, I pray you find strength and hope in your struggles. Remember, God's peace, beyond all comprehension, is there to protect your heart and mind in Christ Jesus. Amen.

Who now rejoice in my sufferings for you, and fill up that which is behind of the afflictions of Christ in my flesh for his body's sake, which is the church: Colossians 1:24 kjv

It is good for me that I have been afflicted; that I might learn thy statutes. Psalm 119:71

Chapter 23

Ministry Beyond Time
Serving with Unyielding Faith

——————— 66 ———————

Now also when I am old and grey-headed, O God, forsaken me not; Until I have shewed ┼thy strength unto this generation, And thy power to everyone that is to come. Psalm 71:18 kjv They shall still bring forth fruit in old age; they shall be fat and flourishing.

Psalm 92:14

——————— 99 ———————

As At 72 years old, my life continues to be a testament to faith, dedication, and service to the Lord. My passion for ministry remains undiminished as I lead congregations, preach the gospel, travel the world, and mentor new ministers.

I start with meditation, prayer, preaching, and caring for my congregation each day. Guiding them with love and wisdom, I share the gospel's eternal truths from the pulpit, inspiring others to seek Jesus Christ.

In quiet moments, I eagerly delve into His Word, finding treasures of wisdom to share with those seeking spiritual growth. The pulpit and the place of worship have become places of learning and spiritual development, where I pass on the knowledge gained from a lifetime of ministry.

The call to travel to distant lands and diverse cultures still beckons me. In Nigeria, South Africa, and Kenya, I work to strengthen fellowship and unity among congregations, spreading the message of love, grace, and redemption without borders.

Mentoring aspiring ministers and preparing them for pastoral duties is not just a duty, but a joyous part of my ministry. Investing in the next generation of shepherds, I pass on the torch of faith and service, guiding others toward discipleship and dedication to God's kingdom. It's a privilege to see them grow and serve.

As I look back on my missionary journeys to Kenya, South Africa, and Nigeria, I recall the powerful impact of God's work in the lives of those we encountered. Miraculous healings, signs, and wonders manifested, touching hearts and transforming communities.

As I approach the conclusion of my long-distance travels, I eagerly anticipate embarking on a meaningful spiritual pilgrimage back to Africa.

This upcoming journey holds great significance as it signifies more than just a physical return; it represents a profound reconnection to the collective spiritual fabric of the global body of Christ. It's a heartfelt opportunity to reinforce our bonds, nurture our shared faith, and lay the groundwork for a future filled with unity, understanding, and mutual support.

"Psalm 103:1-5 (KJV) *says, "Bless the Lord, O my soul: and all that is within me, bless his holy name. Bless the Lord, O my soul, and forget not all his benefits: Who forgiveth all thine iniquities; who healeth all thy diseases; Who redeemeth thy life from destruction; who crowneth thee with lovingkindness and tender mercies; Who satisfieth thy mouth with good things; so that thy youth is renewed like the eagle's."*

Psalm 104:33 (KJV) states, *"I will sing unto the Lord as long as I live: I will sing praise to my God while I have my being."* Psalm 145:4-7 (KJV) declares, *"One generation shall praise thy works to another and declare thy mighty acts. I will speak of the glorious honor of thy majesty and wondrous works. And men shall speak of the might of thy terrible acts: and I will declare thy greatness. They shall abundantly utter the memory of their great goodness and sing of their righteousness."*

These scriptures remind me to bless and praise the Lord at all times for His countless blessings and mighty works.

"…I freed myself from resentment and anger. I let go of the chains and the shackles of the past…".

Chapter 24

Confrontation and Forgiveness

―――――― 66 ――――――

For if ye forgive men their trespasses, your heavenly father will also forgive you.

Matthew 6:14

―――――― 99 ――――――

In 2004, during our tent ministry in Duhaney Park, Kingston, Jamaica, the menacing threat of Hurricane Ivan forced us to dismantle the tent, a task that carried the weight of the impending storm. The relief that followed was palpable.

Worried about my father's safety in his risky living situation in Spanish Town, Paul and I took the proactive step of inviting him to stay with us in our apartment in Kingston, ensuring his safety was our top priority.

The aftermath of Hurricane Ivan hurricane Ivan left Kingston in ruins. Even months later, the thought of sending my father back to Spanish Town was too difficult to entertain. Instead, we continued to provide care for him in our apartment.

Living with my father was not easy; the pain inflicted by him in the past brought back memories of misery and the unbearable pain of betrayal. As I stood in my apartment, I felt the weight of the past weighing me down like a mountain. The hurricane's chaos mirrored the internal storm I knew I had to face head-on and resolve for my deliverance.

The years of pain and betrayal I experienced while living with my father in Lluidas Vale cast a shadow over me. As I stood in the quietness of my apartment, the weight of the past loomed large, mirroring the chaos of the external hurricane and prompting a necessary confrontation with the past.

Confronting my father about the pain he had

inflicted upon me was a critical moment. I remember the day, time and even the moment I confronted my father about the pain he inflicted on me. He couldn't speak due to multiple strokes, but his tears and touch said more than words ever could. In that agonizing moment, I sensed his unspoken plea for forgiveness, a silent acknowledgment of his remorse.

In the aftermath of this emotional reckoning, a sense of peace washed over me—a peace born of forgiveness and acceptance.

After confronting him, I found peace through forgiveness for the first time since the day I met my father. By forgiving him, I freed myself from resentment and anger. I let go of the chains and the shackles of the past. Forgiving him was more for my healing than for him.

By forgiving him, I choose not to be held back by the pain he caused. I embraced a path of inner healing and redemption. Caring for my father and forgiving him revealed my character and strength. It showed me a path toward grace, restoration, and inner peace.

I remembered Jesus' words to his disciples in Matthew 6:15; *"but if you do not forgive men their trespasses, neither will your Father forgive your trespasses."*

Conclusion

A Legacy of Faith and Service

As I reflect on my life and service, one truth stands clear: God's promise to me in 1990 - *"You shall not die, but live to declare the works of God."*

My greatest passion has been witnessing the transformative power of the gospel and embracing the world with the message of Jesus Christ. My experiences have not only guided my path, fueled my spirit, and strengthened my faith, but also filled me with hope and inspiration for the future.

From quiet prayers at dawn to powerful sermons from the pulpit, the message of love, redemption, and salvation has not only filled my heart and soul, but also brought me immense joy and fulfillment. The call to share the good news of Jesus Christ has driven me to walk in faith, speak with conviction, and serve with humility, uplifting and encouraging me in my journey.

Embracing the globe with the gospel has broadened my vision, deepened my compassion, and strengthened my resolve and love for humanity. From the bustling streets of New York to the serene villages of Africa, I have seen the transformative power of grace, the language of faith, and God's boundless love for all creation. These experiences have not only enriched my faith but also deepened my understanding of the universal appeal of the gospel.

The journey of global ministry has been a pilgrimage of faith and courage. It is a testament to the power of obedience and service in reaching hearts and souls with the message of salvation.

My faith has woven a tapestry of resilience and trust in God's providence through illness, adversity, triumph, and joy. My challenges have refined my character, deepened my compassion, and strengthened my resolve to continue my ministry with passion and purpose—to "win the lost at any cost."

Looking to the future with hope and anticipation, I feel immense gratitude for my journey. I am deeply thankful for the opportunities, the challenges that have shaped me, and the people who have walked alongside me. This moment of reflection fills me with a deep conviction in the gospel's power to transform lives, heal hearts, and bring light to the darkest corners of the world.

My passion for preaching the gospel and my mission to spread the message of Jesus Christ globally have kept my faith strong and my spirit vibrant. My mission is not just to share the gospel, but to see lives transformed, communities united, and hope restored. This is the driving force behind my ministry.

I hope my life and ministry will be a testament to the enduring power of faith, God's transformative grace, and the boundless reach of love that unites humanity through the gospel of Jesus Christ.

As I prepare for succession, may Christ's light shine brightly through me, guiding others— especially the younger generation- as I walk the path of faith and service. I desire to inspire hearts to seek the truth, embrace God's grace and faithfulness, and live out the mission of Jesus' love that defines the gospel.

With grateful hearts and unwavering faith, let's journey onward together. Let's spread the message of hope, healing, and salvation to the ends of the earth, fulfilling Christ's great commission in Matthew 28:16-20 to "go therefore." For the glory of God and the transformation of souls, I will continue to go until I can go no more!

Now therefore give me this mountain, whereof the Lord spake in that day; for thou heardest in that day how the Anakims were there, and that the cities were great and fenced: if so be the Lord will be with me, then I shall be able to drive them out, as the Lord said Joshua 14:12 KJV Amen!

Sermons

Sermon # 1 Sermon
Why do I suffer

---- 66 ----

"It is good for me that I have been afflicted; that I might learn thy statutes."

Psalm 119:71

---- ----

Have you ever thought about the phrase, "It is good for me that I have been afflicted"? At first, it seems strange. Who welcomes pain and suffering? Yet, the psalmist reveals a deeper truth – the power of adversity to transform us.

We live in a world filled with challenges. Illness, loss, and life's burdens test our resolve and faith. In these moments, the psalmist reminds us that suffering can brings us closer to God and help us understand His Word better.

When we face affliction, we learn and internalize God's statutes. Just as a refiner's fire purifies gold, suffering refines our hearts and minds, leading to spiritual growth and enlightenment.

God weaves suffering with grace and redemption into the tapestry of our lives. Through trials, we come to know God's goodness, faithfulness, and unwavering love, even in our darkest days.

Remember that God is always present when life's storms rage and adversity overwhelms us. He whispers in our pleasures, speaks in our consciences, and shouts in our pains. Through suffering, we see God's mighty hand guiding, sustaining, and transforming us into vessels of His grace and mercy.

So, if you are suffering, do not despair. Turn to God through His Word, seek solace in His promises, and let His love light your path. Embrace the blessing in suffering, knowing it brings you closer to God and His transformative power. Find strength in trials, hope in afflictions, and faith in God's constant presence. Amen.

From my sermon at Citadel of Hope International Ministries – Spanish Town, Jamaica – May 19th, 2024.

Sermon #2 God's Plan for Me
Understanding Jeremiah 29:11

As we explore God's Word, let's set aside our preconceived ideas and uncover the deep truths within the sacred text. Jeremiah 29:11 is often misunderstood as a promise of immediate deliverance from suffering. However, this scripture speaks to a deeper reality – the call to thrive amidst trials.

The prophet Jeremiah's words to the Israelites during their exile remind us of God's unfailing love and sovereign plan, even in dark times. The Israelites were in captivity, facing the consequences of their disobedience and enduring the harsh realities of exile. False prophets like Hananiah promised them quick relief, but Jeremiah's message was different. God's plan was not about immediate deliverance but about enduring faith and perseverance. The core of Jeremiah 29:11 is a call to seek peace and prosperity in the land of their captivity and to pray for the welfare of the nation that held them captive. This message was a radical call to trust God's providence and embrace His plan, even when it didn't align with their desires. The Israelites hoped for a quick return to their homeland, but they learned their exile would last seventy years – beyond their lifetimes. This revelation was crushing, yet God's promise of a prosperous future remained a beacon of hope in their dark circumstances.

In our trials, we are called to embrace Jeremiah 29:11 with a new perspective. Instead of expecting immediate relief from suffering, let's seek to thrive amid our trials. Let's persevere through pain and adversity, trusting God's plan is unfolding with divine wisdom.

The path to true growth and spiritual maturity is often filled with hardships and challenges. It is through enduring life's storms with unwavering faith that we discover deep joy and peace. Let's not shy away from difficulties. Instead, let's face them with courage, knowing God's grace sustains us and

His promise of hope shines brightly even in our suffering.

Listen to me today! Hold onto Jeremiah 29:11 in your struggles. This verse is not a promise of immediate relief but a gospel assurance that God will give you hope and strength to endure. May your faith grow stronger, your spirit lift, and your heart filled with confidence that God's plan for you is one of prosperity and growth, even in trials.

Let us pray:

Heavenly Father, in our trials and tribulations, we come before You with humble hearts, seeking Your strength and guidance. Grant us the courage to face our challenges, the wisdom to understand Your plan, and the faith to trust in Your unfailing love. May Your presence bring comfort and peace, helping us thrive in adversity and find joy in our faith journey. We lift our burdens to You, knowing Your promises are true and grace is enough.

May the peace of God, which surpasses all understanding, guard your hearts and minds in Christ Jesus. Amen.

By God's Grace I Stand

From my sermon at Citadel of Hope International Ministries Spanish Town, Jamaica – May 23rd, 2024.

Sermon # 3
Rizpah and the Buzzards
2 Samuel 21:1-14, 2 Samuel 3:7-12

In our world, tragedy is all too common. We see it on the news, and sometimes it hits close to home. Many people in the Bible also experienced tragedies, including a woman named Rizpah. But who was she, and what did she go through? And how can her story help us today?

Rizpah's story begins in a dispute between two men in the Bible. She was one of King Saul's concubines. After Saul's death, his son Ish-Bosheth became king over Gilad with the help of Abner, Saul's army commander. A long-standing war between the houses of Saul and David ensued. Abner, who supported Saul's side, accused Ish-Bosheth of sleeping with Rizpah. This accusation angered Abner, who then helped Ish-Bosheth become king. Realizing God's promise of all Israel to David, Abner made a treaty with David but was later killed by Joab.

Rizpah later faced an unthinkable tragedy. As a widow with little power, her sons were chosen to be sacrificed for an oath broken years before. Unable to stop the death sentence, her two sons were hanged in Gibeah of Saul. Rizpah stayed by their side for months, protecting their bodies from birds and wild animals.

To better understand Rizpah's Story, we need to go back to Joshua 9. Joshua, Moses's successor, led the Israelites to the Promised Land, overcoming enemies with God's help. The Gibeonites, who tricked the Israelites into a peace treaty, were actually their neighbors. Saul later broke this oath by killing the Gibeonites, leading to a three-year famine. The Gibeonites demanded the sacrifice of seven of Saul's male descendants, including Rizpah's sons.

Rizpah's story is one of grief and sorrow. She watched her innocent sons die for their father's sins, enduring unimaginable pain. Like Rizpah, many today face tragedies that seem unbearable. Rizpah's grief continued for months, but through her dedication, her sons received a proper burial, and the drought ended.

From Rizpah's Story, we learn three important lessons:

1. God can use our tragedies for good, as seen in the restoration of Israel after her sons' sacrifice.
2. There is a time to grieve, as Rizpah did by staying with her sons' bodies.
3. We have the strength to endure, even in the face of unimaginable hardships, just as Rizpah remained strong in protecting her children.

Rizpah's story is a testament to her strength and love for her children. She remained faithful in the midst of tragedy, and God saw her and brought restoration. God remains in control in our tragedies and can provide comfort and restoration, just as He did for Rizpah. Let us take courage from Rizpah's example and trust in God's faithfulness in our times of sorrow. Amen!

From my sermon preached at Restoration Ministries Toronto on April 20th, 2024

Sermon # 4 Praise Him Through the Storm
Acts 16:16-40

Let's dive into the Story of Paul and Silas and how they showed the power of praise in overcoming trials. Life is full of challenges, but we can find victory through praising God.

Paul and Silas were unjustly arrested, beaten, and thrown into prison for helping a slave girl. Despite their dire situation, they chose to respond with praise and worship. This decision led to their miraculous deliverance and the salvation of the jailer and his household.

What stands out is the unwavering praise Paul and Silas offered to God amidst their trials. They were not just facing a minor inconvenience; they were in a life-threatening predicament. Despite being severely beaten and confined in a dark, filthy prison cell, they chose to focus on God and offer Him praise.

The example of Paul and Silas teaches us that no matter how challenging our circumstances, there is always a reason to praise God. Our worship is not dependent on our situation but on the unchanging character of God. He is eternally good, loving, and faithful, even when our surroundings are bleak. By praising God in our trials, we acknowledge His sovereignty and express our trust in His ability to see us through.

Our perspective changes when we shift our focus from our problems to God and His goodness. Instead of being overwhelmed by our challenges, we become attuned to God's presence and His capacity to help us. This shift can significantly impact how we navigate our trials. Instead of succumbing to fear and hopelessness, we can face our difficulties with faith and confidence in God's ability to turn things for our benefit.

Our praise can change the spiritual atmosphere around us. Just as Paul and Silas experienced a supernatural intervention through their worship, our praises can invite God's presence into our situations. While we may not witness earthquakes and prison doors opening, our worship is a powerful weapon against the enemy's attempts to keep us in fear and despair.

As we raise our voices in praise, we declare our trust in God's deliverance and proclaim our victory in Christ. This act can break the chains of fear and hopelessness, creating an environment where God's presence is felt. Let us draw strength from Paul and Silas and commit to praising God in all circumstances, knowing our worship can bring about miraculous breakthroughs.

Over the years, as I faced several strokes, my constant was walking the floor and sometimes dragging myself, praising God through the storm. The doctors later told me I am likely alive today because I stayed in motion during these strokes. This personal testimony underscores the power of praise in times of trouble and its profound impact on our mental and physical well-being. Let us take this lesson to heart and continue to praise God, even in life's storms.

Perspectives

MY EXPERIENCE WITH BISHOP DR. LETITIA E. MCPHERSON

I have known my friend Bishop Dr. Letitia McPherson (Citadel of Hope International and Ministries Restoration Evangelistic Ministries of Canada) for approximately 40 years. Dr. McPherson loves the Lord with all her heart. She is a person of great influence, a mighty woman of valour, and a woman of remarkable courage in the face of danger and life challenges.

Dr. McPherson is an exceptional shepherd to God's flock. She desires to see others reach their full potential of honour and excellence. She is a dynamic Bible teacher and preacher with excellent communication skills. Her Doctor of Divinity (M.Div..) level of education is evident in her teaching and preaching. Those listening to her sermons notice her passion for the Lord and His Word. Dr. McPherson is also a prophetess who speaks forth the Word of God with precision and without compromise.

As an Apostle and Bishop, Dr. McPherson oversees many churches. She is able to effectively and successfully oversee multiple programs simultaneously. She has a natural gift for administration. She takes pride in ensuring things are always done right, thus bringing honour and glory to God. Dr. McPherson writes church constitutions, church Policies & Procedures manuals, and ordains Ministers, Pastors, Bishops and Reverends for the work of the ministry.

Dr. McPherson is highly anointed, gifted and talented. She is also a counsellor whose guidance, insight and empathy have been invaluable to others during difficult times.

We have all been created for a purpose, and it is not until we realize, embrace, and walk in our God-given-calling that we begin to live a life of fulfilment and enrichment. Dr. McPherson has realized that she was indeed called by God, and therefore walks in her God-given calling and purpose with a heart of gracefulness, integrity and honour.

She is also a songwriter, singer and author. Her most recent song, entitled, "god's Grace I Stand", coincides with the title of her newly written book: By GOD'S GRACE I STAND - MY FAITH WALK

As a Christian woman of God, Dr. McPhersons heart desires to be more like Jesus and to walk in the will of God. Dr. McPherson's experiences presented in this book will help everyone, from individuals to church members to the community. Dr. McPherson depends on God more than herself. Her own personal faith walk has given her the authority to write this book as an encouragement to you and your walk of faith.

-Sr. Pastor Wendy Burnett, M.Div.

Bethel Restoration Ministries

Bishop Dr. Letitia McPherson's Prolific, Prophetic, Healing, and Breakthrough Worldwide Ministry

For the past 29 years, I have had the privilege of knowing this anointed mighty woman of God and witnessing firsthand the profound impact of her prolific, prophetic, healing, and breakthrough ministry on a global scale. Dr. Mac's (as she is affectionately called – by me) unwavering dedication to spreading the message of faith, healing, and transformation has touched the lives of countless individuals and communities around the world.

Through her prophetic insights and spiritual guidance, Dr. Mac has provided hope, encouragement, and direction to those seeking divine intervention and clarity in their lives. Her ability to connect with people on a deep, spiritual level (hugs included) transcends boundaries and cultural differences, fostering a sense of unity and shared purpose among believers.

In the realm of healing, Dr. McPherson's ministry has been a beacon of light for those grappling with physical, emotional, and spiritual challenges. Her prayers, prophetic declarations and anointing have brought about countless miraculous healings and restoration, instilling faith and renewed hope and strength in the hearts of the afflicted – too many to mention here.

Furthermore, Dr. McPherson's emphasis on breakthrough and overcoming obstacles has empowered individuals to rise above limitations and embrace their full potential. Her teachings on faith, perseverance, and the power of prayer have inspired many to press on in the face of adversity and achieve remarkable victories in their lives.

As I reflect on the transformative impact of Dr. Letitia McPherson's prolific ministry, I am filled with gratitude for her unwavering commitment to spreading light, hope, and healing across the globe. Her work continues to inspire and uplift souls, leaving a legacy of faith, love, and empowerment. This woman of great faith who carries an anointing that oozes from her very soul, is truly, "a Woman with a Word and a Testimony." She wholeheartedly does "Stand by God's Grace."

Bishop Seymore Phori
Bloemfontein South Africa
Mount as Eagles Ministries

Mama McPherson's Anointed Ministry in Ogun State, Nigeria

In the village of Ogun State, Nigeria, Mama McPherson is a woman whom God has used significantly to impact the lives of the people in this community. We look forward to her missionary visits with great anticipation and pray always for her safe return.

Over the years, Mama McPherson's ministry has been like a flowing river of anointing and blessings, bringing hope, healing, and transformation to the villagers.

Mama McPherson is a woman who carries the fire of God within her, shining brightly like the morning sun. Her prayers are powerful, and her words carry wisdom that touches the hearts of those who hear them.

She walks with authority and grace, bringing peace and joy to the villagers through her presence.

In matters of healing, Mama Esther's ministry acts as a soothing balm for the sick and afflicted in the community. Many individuals who have suffered from various illnesses and troubles have sought Mama McPherson's prayers and anointing, resulting in divine healing and restoration.

The villagers testify to the miracles that God has performed through Mama McPherson, praising Him for her life and ministry.

Furthermore, Mama McPherson imparts teachings on faith, love, and the power of prayer to the people. She encourages them to trust in God's promises and stand firm in their faith.

Her messages inspire hope and courage, motivating the villagers to live their lives with faith and purpose.

As I reflect on Mama McPherson's ministry and the profound impact it has had on the community in Ogun State, I see the hand of God working through her.

Her anointed ministry serves as an example of light, guiding the villagers towards God's love and grace. Mama McPherson is truly a woman of God, and her legacy of faith and love will continue to shine for generations to come.

Gratefully Yours,
Pastor Moshe Ogunjobi
Glad Tidings House of Praise

My Experience with Rev. Doctor Letitia McPherson A Beacon of Transformation in Jamaican Ministry

My name is Rev. Junior Rutty, and I am honoured to share my encounter with the illustrious Rev. Doctor Letitia McPherson, whose remarkable contributions have profoundly transformed the landscape of ministry in Jamaica. My experience with her has not only been enriching but also a testament to her unwavering dedication to spiritual and social upliftment.

Rev. Dr. McPherson is a visionary leader whose innovative approaches have redefined ministry on our island. Her journey has been one of tireless commitment to fostering community growth, spiritual development, and social justice. Under her guidance, the ministry has evolved to address the contemporary needs of the people while staying rooted in the timeless principles of faith and compassion.

One of the most striking aspects of Rev. Dr. McPherson's ministry is her focus on education and empowerment. She has pioneered numerous programs aimed at uplifting the underprivileged and providing opportunities for personal and professional growth. all of which have had a lasting impact on countless lives.

In addition to her educational endeavours, Rev. Dr. McPherson has been vocal advocate for social justice. She has spearheaded campaigns against domestic violence, substance abuse, and poverty, bringing these critical issues to the forefront of public consciousness. Her efforts have not only provided immediate relief to those in need but have also sparked broader societal change, encouraging a more inclusive and compassionate community.

One of my most memorable experiences with Rev. Dr. McPherson was during a collaborative outreach program with the Assemblies of God in Jamaica. Her ability to connect with people from all walks of life, coupled with her profound empathy and wisdom, was truly inspiring.

As we worked together to impact those in need, I witnessed firsthand the profound impact of her ministry. The gratitude and hope in the eyes of the beneficiaries were a testament to the transformative power of God in her work.

Rev. Dr. McPherson's influence extends beyond the church and community. She has also made significant strides in interfaith dialogue, fostering a spirit of unity and cooperation among different religious groups.

Her efforts have helped to build bridges of understanding and mutual respect, promoting a harmonious coexistence in our diverse society.

In conclusion, Rev. Dr. Letitia McPherson is a beacon of hope and a catalyst for change in Jamaica. Her dedication, compassion, faith and innovative spirit have not only transformed individual lives but have also reshaped the broader landscape of ministry on our island. It has been a privilege to witness and partake in her extraordinary journey, and I am confident that her legacy will continue to inspire and uplift future generations.

Rev. Junior Rutty
Agape Christian Fellowship
85 Market Street, Falmouth, Trelawny

My Experience with Bishop Rev. Dr. Letitia McPherson A Biblical Demonstration of Love

Greetings to all.

This is to state my knowledge of the late Rev. Dr. Paul Anthony McPherson, from the time I met him and his wife, Bishop, Rev, Dr. Letitia McPherson, in October 2016.

On landing in Toronto, I received them as they deplaned in wheelchairs. Immediately, they were taken to the Etobicoke General hospital, where pastor Paul was admitted.

Other tests were done where it was discovered that his cancer had spread. With meticulous care and attention, Bishop Letitia McPherson was looking after her husband, 24/7. She missed nothing. She was "nurse, nurse and nurse" to pastor Paul. She demonstrated true love, in working clothes. In fact, I believe that if it were not for her perspicacious insight in pastor Paul's care, maybe he would have passed much sooner.

On finding a place to live so that she could care for him more freely, she now had more to do. I observed that during this time, pastor Paul's well-being and best interest consumed her. She washed, cooked, cleaned, dressed his wounds, turned him whenever he needed, fed him, carried him, and went beyond what I am able to say.

She would frequently say: I am first Paul's wife and then everything else comes after.

I believe that Jesus Christ cared for Pastor Paul, through her.

I have NEVER seen anyone care for someone with that kind of indefatigable spirit.

Right up until pastor Paul passed, Bishop McPherson was fighting for her husband. Personally, I am deeply moved by this woman's love for her husband. I thought that I knew what love was. Bishop McPherson helped me to understand more deeply that love is "caring endurance" and so much more.

My regrets are that we lost pastor Paul and that others didn't have the opportunity to go to "university love", as I had, in being there most of the time, as she cared for him.

Wanted: more Letitia McPherson(s). I am better off because I have known them. Pastor Paul taught me to have quiet strength. He taught me to face suffering and death with unflinching confidence. He exuded the truth: O death, where is your sting, O death where is your victory? Thanks be to God; we have the victory through Jesus Christ our Lord.

Bishop Letitia McPherson, thanks for your **biblical** demonstration of love. You are a Gem to the body of Christ. Continue to shine forth in this dark world.

Blessings!
Rev. Dr. Gene Archer
Toronto Canada

My Experience with Bishop McPherson

Bishop Doctor Letitia McPherson - what a fascinating human being! Having a demure physique, with nothing to indicate from looking at her, the depth of physical strength that has allowed her to endure and overcome the many health challenges over her lifetime. A powerful woman, you would say, and you would be right.

It wouldn't take you too long in her presence to recognize the indomitable quality of her spirit forged through her faith in God. She has successfully navigated the situations and circumstances in her life, which shows God is unreservedly revealing Himself to her to keep her faith growing.

Dr. McPherson has pastored the Citadel of Hope International Ministries and Restoration Evangelical Ministries of Canada for over forty (40) years. Her devotion to the Word of God, sound thought, pastoral discernment, and a no-nonsensical approach have characterized her ministry. Over the years, this has fostered a heart-warming assurance among her congregation of the Lord's blessing upon and provision for her pastoral calling in a secularized world.

Her influence reaches far beyond her local congregation as her role as Bishop and an effective church leader is evident in her overseeing numerous churches and their programs. Expanding and building up the kingdom of God has been her life's vocation as far as the grace of God allowed.

The apostle Peter stated that God's "divine power has given to us, all things that pertain to life and godliness, through the knowledge of Him who called us by glory and virtue" (2 Peter 1:3). That knowledge is provided by God's written Word (vv. 3-21) and by the experiential nature of our walk with Christ.

Bishop McPherson's book emphasizes the necessity of going to the Bible for our wellspring of knowledge that we may be provided answers from the mind of God, spoken first by His Son, and written down through the inspiration of the Holy Spirit by the apostles, and prophets of the first century (John 14:24-26; 16:12-15; Hebrews 1:2; Ephesians 3:5).

The faith-building realizations experienced by her recognition of the workings of the power of God in her health challenges, tests, and trials, along with the faith built up in her spirit from abiding in the Word of God, provide the conduit for endless possibilities, for grace to be applied to her life. This is helpful for all believers who struggle to know that the good things that have already been laid up for them, as God's grace, are waiting to be appropriated through unwavering faith in Him.

-Reverend Robert Noble,
B. Theology

Testimony by Vivienne - Gordon

Last August (1923), I visited the doctor at Red Hills Mall due to weight loss and frequent urination. Concerned, the doctor referred me to Kingston Public Hospital (KPH), but I expressed my reluctance to go there. Instead, he suggested Andrews Medical. In September, I followed his advice and underwent a sugar test, revealing high levels that required insulin treatment to manage.

During the examination, the doctor noticed a tumour on my breast and promptly referred me to a Breast Oncologist. In October, I met with the specialist who conducted a biopsy, confirming the presence of breast cancer.

Following the diagnosis, I underwent X-rays and blood work, with mostly positive results except for elevated blood sugar levels. On November 17th, 2023, during my scheduled appointment, I was afraid and uncertain. However, amidst the anxiety, I heard the comforting voice of the Lord assuring me that I was not given a spirit of fear but of love, power and a sound mind. As I prepared for surgery, a nurse offered a heartfelt prayer, bringing a sense of peace and reassurance.

Supported by the prayers and love of my family, I faced the surgical procedure with faith and courage. Despite the challenges ahead, I held onto the belief that God was by my side, guiding me through each step of the journey. In the operating room, surrounded by medical staff, I felt a sense of calm and assurance that only divine presence can provide.

Following the successful surgery to remove my right breast and the placement of drain bottles, I was discharged on Saturday and sent home. Remarkably, I experienced minimal pain and could move around as usual, a testament to God's amazing grace and healing power.

Reflecting on this journey, I give all glory to God for His miraculous intervention and unwavering presence throughout the process. His love and grace carried me through moments of uncertainty, reminding me of His faithfulness and the power of prayer. I stand in awe of His goodness and thank Him for the healing and strength He has bestowed upon me. Amen and Amen.

Vivienne - Wignal-Gordon Kingston, Jamaica

Testimony of Edina M. Bayne

My testimony is of the Lord, God, the Almighty and His unchanging grace. I testify that He is the good, all-knowing deliverer, giver and sustainer of life, and that He showed himself mighty, once again, on Tuesday, December 5th, 2023, in the suburbs of the West Island of Montreal, Canada. I am here today because He kept me alive after suffering a stroke on the left side of my brain.

Tuesday, December 5th, 2023, started like every other early weekday morning for the past five years. By 7 am I would have already been awake for more than an hour, since this was a day for early individual prayer – awake but not out of bed. I had already gone through my morning stretches and calisthenics before getting out of bed, slowly.

I was experiencing some tingling or numbness to my right hand, forearm and biceps, which I attributed to sleeping awkwardly. I attempted to massage and stimulate the forearm and fingers but to no avail. I considered the time-period too long to be massaging and stimulating without any noticeable change, so I decided to get up and out of bed anyway. I sat up, swung my left leg over the side of the bed, turned my hip, followed with the right leg, and proceeded to stand.

While standing, I continued to flex and extend my fingers and shake out my arm, but it was in my attempt to take my first step that I realized that something was dreadfully wrong. I moved my left leg forward, but my right leg remained glued to where I had placed it; it refused to follow. My affected brain had lost awareness of where the right leg was, so it could not send instructions. My first and instinctive thought was to say this, ""Lord, is this the day that I die?"" I did not linger long in that space; because I was alive, I continued to be actively engaged in this experience.

I was alone in the house, so there was no evident help within proximity. I called my daughter, who was on her way to work, but did not get a response – I just wanted to inform family, especially because I have a USA phone number in Canada, and I wasn't sure that 911 worked. I then called a cousin and told her to call, just in case, however, I proceeded to call and did succeed. I informed the responder that the right side of my body was not working, where I was in the house, and how they might gain access since I was nowhere near the front door and was not sure I could get there.

Using the right leg as a prop, and depending on the muscular strength in the left leg, I got to the bathroom, put a warm house jacket on; emptied a small cross-body bag and stacked it with a credit card, about $40 Canadian, and an ID; proceeded to the front door, located the key and placed it in the keyhole, dragged a winter coat out of the cupboard and waited for help to come.

I'm sharing these details because there is glory in the fact that I continued to use whatever parts of me were functional – my brain, and my ability to think critically, and to organize certainly were working. I did not panic; I did not begin to speak in tongues; I did not "pray" as we prayer. There was no Hezekiah moment, I simply trusted God and knew that He was totally in control at that moment, no matter the eventuality.

Fire and Rescue arrived, hooked me up to oxygen, bundled me up and took me on a gurney down the flights of stairs, into the ambulance and whisked me away to the L'Hôpital du Sacre Coeur de Montréal. Though French is my second language, when one is ill or under any kind of stress or trauma the comfortable, natural thing to do is to revert to her mother tongue. A brain scan done in the Emergency Department (ED) confirmed that I had stroked, but the cause was not evident because the affected part of the brain was already repairing itself.

Once they got me out of the ED and into a room I did not concentrate on the illness, but rather on the unfinished tasks that I had. Realizing that I could use my extremities – that my fingers were functioning – I asked my daughter to bring me my laptop; there was a book to be completed. On December 10th, five days after being diagnosed with a left-brain stroke (right side affected, and I am righthanded), I embarked upon the completion of my most recent work ""The Father Who Mothered Me"", a book about success, resilience, and independence of a daughter raised by a single father. I had a publishing deadline for December 15th – book cover to be confirmed and approved along with finetuning and uploading. That deadline was met, to the glory of God.

Once my headphones were brought to me and network was stable, I picked up my Wall Builders presence, and participation in The Kingdom Series while still in hospital. My declaration of God in my situation, constantly speaking to the medical staff that the cause can't be found because God has fixed it, was an inspiration for the team. Declaring that I would walk out of their facilities, and I did... I have a clean bill of health – perfect report in all crucial areas, no high blood pressure, no cholesterol issues, no heart arrhythmia, no sugar diabetes, yet I had a medical incident. The doctors were compelled to declare, ""We have done all that we can to find a cause, and we have not, so we must sign off on your records, "No Known Cause" I'm in rehab and physiotherapy, working my way back to my baseline. My physical goal is to run, and if I can't run to walk, my next 5K race is by January of 2025. I continue to run this race of life, to the Glory of God!

Sermon Notes - Nuggets
My Story isn't Over

And the keeper of the prison awaking out of his sleep, and seeing the prison doors open, he drew out his sword, and would have killed himself, supposing that the prisoners had been fled. But Paul cried with a loud voice, saying, Do thyself no harm: for we are all here. Then he called for a light, and sprang in, and came trembling, and fell down before Paul and Silas, And brought them out, and said, Sirs, what must I do to be saved? And they said, Believe on the Lord Jesus Christ, and thou shalt be saved, and thy house. And they spake unto him the word of the Lord, and to all that were in his house. And he took them the same hour of the night, and washed their stripes; and was baptized, he and all his, straightway. The depths of our faith are often revealed in times of trial and darkness. The midnight moments of our lives test our resolve and illuminate the strength of our relationship with God. In Acts 16, Paul and Silas show unwavering faith and praise in the face of adversity.

SCRIPTURE: ACTS 16:16-32

JEREMIAH 29:11; "For I know the thoughts that I think toward you, saith the LORD, thoughts of peace, and not of evil, to give you an expected end."

POINT 1: TRUSTING IN GOD'S WILL

- The safest place we can be is within the will of God, where His purpose and plan for our lives unfold.

- God's will may not always lead to comfort and ease, but it is where we find true fulfillment and spiritual growth.

- God's goal is our sanctification and transformation, shaping us into vessels of His grace and love.

POINT 2: FINDING HOPE IN MIDNIGHT MOMENTS

- Paul and Silas, amidst their imprisonment and suffering, chose to pray and praise God at midnight, showing unwavering faith.

- Midnight symbolizes the darkest hour of our lives, where uncertainty and hardship prevail, but also where God's light and deliverance shine brightest.

- In our midnight experiences, we can find solace and strength in knowing that God's presence and power are always with us.

POINT 3: BEARING WITNESS THROUGH TRIALS

- The testimony of Paul and Silas in prison led to the conversion of the jailer and his household, illustrating the power of faith in trials.

- Our faith and praise in times of darkness serve as a powerful witness to those around us, drawing others closer to God's love.

- As God's chosen vessels, we are called to shine His light in the darkest of places, sharing His love and hope with a world in need of salvation.

Just as Paul and Silas found strength and hope

in their midnight hour, we too can trust in God's faithfulness and provision in our trials. Our story is still being written by the author of life, and He holds the pen to our future. Let us continue to praise Him in every season, knowing that our story isn't over yet, and that He who began a good work in us will bring it to completion.

Looking unto Jesus the author and finisher of our faith, who for the joy that was set before him endured the cross, despising the shame, and is set down at the right hand of the throne of God. Hebrews 12:2

By God's Grace I Stand

Scripture Reading:

"For in him we live, and move, and have our being; as certain also of your own poets have said, for we are also his offspring."

Acts 17:28 kjv

"But and if ye suffer for righteousness' sake, happy are ye: and be not afraid of their terror, neither be troubled;"

1 Peter 3:14 kjv

"Be careful about nothing; but in everything by prayer and supplication with thanksgiving let your requests be made known unto God."

Philippians 4:6

www.ingramcontent.com/pod-product-compliance
Lightning Source LLC
Chambersburg PA
CBHW060341170426
43202CB00014B/2842